The Viking
Eastern Baltic

Marika Mägi

ARCHUMANITIES PRESS

Translated by Piret Ruustal.
Financially supported by institutional research funding IUT (IUT18-8) of the Estonian Ministry of Education and Research.

British Library Cataloguing in Publication Data
A catalogue record for this book is available from the British Library

ISBN (print): 9781641890977
e-ISBN (PDF): 9781641890984
e-ISBN (EPUB): 9781641890991

www.arc-humanities.org
Printed and bound by CPI Group (UK) Ltd, Croydon, CR0 4YY

Contents

List of Illustrations

Figures

Maps

Map 1. Map of the historical districts of the Eastern Baltic.

Introduction

The very latest research shows that the Viking influence on the eastern coasts of the Baltic Sea and today's Russia was at least as significant as their westward—and much better known—influence in the North Atlantic. At any rate, based on current information, raids in the Baltic Sea were earlier than the Vikings' first forays into Western Europe. This book discusses the impact of the Viking Age Scandinavians on the Eastern Baltic region—an impact entailing variously pillaging, raids, military and commercial cooperation.

The modern-day Baltic States (Estonia, Latvia, and Lithuania) are habitually perceived as a single, culturally uniform region, a perception that is routinely projected back into the past. Nothing can be further from the truth. The region in fact falls into two distinct halves, both linguistically and in terms of religion; in terms of history their paths have diverged dramatically and did not converge again until the twentieth century. A one-time superpower, Lithuania takes pride in its former status as a Grand Duchy, whereas the rest of the Eastern Baltic, far from being a homogeneous entity, has time and again found itself governed by an assortment of political structures.

Barely a century ago, Finland was also viewed as being part of the region, as one of four Baltic countries. Even today, Estonia has a closer cultural affinity with Finland than with its other neighbours; Latvia and Lithuania, on the other hand, enjoy a strong bond based on linguistic kinship and a shared cultural identity.

During the Viking Age the situation was presumably similar to the way it is today, and it is safe to say there was never any common "Baltic" archaeological culture covering the present-day Baltic countries (Map 1).

Instead, two diverse regions can be identified in the Eastern Baltic. The Baltic Finnic Iron Age culture thrived in the northern half of the Eastern Baltic and the northwestern part of today's Russia; the Balts' culture spread in the southern half, also embracing the northeastern areas of today's Poland and part of Belarus.

Likewise, the term "Baltic" is used differently in different countries and languages. Archaeologists within the Baltic States themselves apply the term exclusively to ethnic Balts, whereas the rest of the world, Finland included, extends it to all three modern Baltic States. Similarly, the word "Finnic" (or "Finnish" in earlier publications) can stand for the Baltic Finnic culture as a whole or can (erroneously) be designated just for modern Finland. So it often happens that Estonia falls into an academic no-man's-land, put in a confusing position where it is unclear whether the region should identify with the Baltic or Finnic/Finnish culture.

An absolutely fundamental distinction therefore runs through this book which juxtaposes the "Baltic Finnic", referring to the people who lived in the territories of modern Finland and Estonia as well as the northwestern part of Russia, and "Baltic" peoples, denoting exclusively ethnic Balts, inhabitants of what is now Latvia and Lithuania. In the Iron Age, today's Latvia was divided between the Baltic Finnic and the Baltic ethnic groups. In the southern parts of the Eastern Baltic, at that period, other ethnic groups could also be found (Semgallians, Cours, and others) in what is now Latvia and Lithuania.

To fully understand the region's history, we cannot underestimate the diverse role of maritime communication in the Eastern Baltic. For maritime culture to thrive, the most important prerequisites are a long coastline together with fertile lands inland to provide sufficient resources to support and sustain human settlement along the coastal areas.

The shores of both Finland and Estonia are rugged, deeply indented, and dotted with hundreds of small islands; the Latvian and Lithuanian coasts are, conversely, relatively straight and, often, with no islands at all. Furthermore, Finland boasts a large number of lakes connected by rivers, whereas Estonia borders on the east with the sizeable Lake Peipus and Lake Pskov. Present-day Estonia has a sea border 3794 km (2358 miles) in length; Latvia's coast stretches 531 km (330 miles), and Lithuania's is just 99 km (62 miles) long, of which only a stretch of about forty kilometres faces the open seas. Historically, Lithuania was entirely landlocked.

This book focuses on the Viking Age which in the Eastern Baltic covered the period of 800 to 1000/1050 CE. Popular literature in this region frequently refers to the "Distinct [or Own] Viking Age of Estonia/Latvia/Lithuania" and is considered to last from the eleventh to the twelfth centuries. Such sentiments are chiefly based on written sources which, understandably, concern themselves more with the later centuries than with the ninth or tenth centuries, and should therefore be taken with a pinch of salt. Even so, the final chapter of the book provides a brief overview of the period immediately following the Viking Age. Sometimes the entire period to 1200 is considered to be part of the Iron Age, though the period prior to 800 to 1000/1050 CE can also be broken down into the Late Iron Age, the Migration Period (from ca. 450 CE) and the Pre-Viking Period from ca. 550. So, in this book, some discussion of Iron Age features corresponds to what in other parts of Europe comprise the early Middle Ages.

Primary Sources Cited

Adam of Bremen. *History of the Archbishops of Hamburg–Bremen.* Translated with an introduction and notes by Francis J. Tschan. Records of Western Civilization, Sources and Studies 53. New York: Columbia University Press, 1959.

The Chronicle of Novgorod 1016–1471. Translated from the Russian by Robert Michell and Nevill Forbes. Camden Society, Third Series 25. London: Royal Historical Society, 1914.

Drevneskandinavskiye istochniki. Drevnyaya Rus´ v svete zarubezhnyh istochnikov. Hrestomatiya. Edited by Tatjana N. Jackson, I. G. Konovalov, and A. V. Podosinov. 5 vols. Moskva: Rossiyskaya Akademiya Nauk, 2009.

Göngu-Hrolfs Saga. Translated by Hermann Pálsson and Paul Edwards. Edinburgh: Canongate, 1980.

Henricus Lettus. *The Chronicle of Henry of Livonia.* Translated and with a new introduction and notes by James A. Brundage. Records of Western Civilization. New York: Columbia University Press, 2003.

A History of Norway and the Passion and Miracles of the Blessed Olafr. Translated by Devra Kunin. London: Viking Society for Northern Research, 2001.

Knytlinga Saga: The History of the Kings of Denmark. Translated by Hermann Pálsson and Paul Edwards. Odense: Odense University Press, 1986.

The Pskov 3rd Chronicle. Edited and translated by David Savignac. Crofton: Beowulf, 2015.

Rimbert. *Anskar, the Apostle of the North, 801–865, Translated from the Vita Anskarii by Bishop Rimbert, his Fellow Missionary and Successor.* Translated by Charles H. Robinson. London: SPCK, 1921.

The Russian Primary Chronicle: Laurentian Text. Translated and edited by Samuel Hazzard Cross and Olgerd P. Sherbowitz-Wetzor. Mediaeval Academy of America Publications, 60. Cambridge, MA: Mediaeval Academy of America, 1953.

The Saga of Magnús the Good. Heimskringla. History of the Kings of Norway by Snorri Sturluson. Translated with introduction and notes by Lee M. Hollander, 538–76. Austin: University of Texas Press, 1995.

The Saga of Óláf Tryggvason. Heimskringla. History of the Kings of Norway by Snorri Sturluson. Translated with introduction and notes by Lee M. Hollander, 144–244. Austin: University of Texas Press, 1995.

The Saga of the Ynglings. Heimskringla. History of the Kings of Norway by Snorri Sturluson. Translated with introduction and notes by Lee M. Hollander, 6–50. Austin: University of Texas Press, 1995.

The Saga of Yngvar the Traveller. Translated by Peter Tunstall, 2005. https://web.archive.org/web/20110726051430/http://www.oe.eclipse.co.uk/nom/Yngvar.htm, accessed September 28, 2018.

Saxo Grammaticus. *Gesta Danorum. The History of the Danes*. Edited by K. Friis-Jensen, translated by P. Fisher. 2 vols. Oxford Medieval Texts. Oxford: Clarendon Press, 2015.

Snorri Sturluson. *Saint Óláf's Saga. Heimskringla. History of the Kings of Norway by Snorri Sturluson*. Translated with introduction and notes by Lee M. Hollander, 245–537. Austin: University of Texas Press, 1995.

The Story of Burnt Njal. Translated by Sir George Webbe Dasent. London: Aldine, 1960.

Sverissaga—The Saga of King Sverri of Norway. https://web.
archive.org/web/20160730171928/http://www.northvegr.org/
sagas%20annd%20epics/kings%20sagas/the%20saga%20
of%20king%20sverri%20of%20norway/index.html, accessed
September 28, 2018.

Ynglingatal, http://skaldic.abdn.ac.uk/db.php?id=1440&if=de-
fault&table=text, accessed September 28, 2018.

Acknowledgements

I wish here to record my gratitude to the translation work of
Piret Ruustal and the financial support of the Estonian Ministry of Education and Research (institutional research funding
IUT 18-8), and to the advice and assistance of the anonymous
readers and the staff of Arc Humanities Press. I hope in this
book to entice more people interested in the Viking Age to
turn their gaze eastwards.

Chapter 1

Different Cultures, Different Modes of Communication

Archaeologists in the Eastern Baltic recognize a great diversity of archaeological cultures present during the Iron Age. Cultural and social differences play an important role in understanding Viking Age maritime communication. It would, however, take up too much space to present a comprehensive overview of current knowledge in this field, so let us therefore highlight particular characteristic phenomena that define the division of the Viking-Age Eastern Baltic into two distinct worlds: that of the Baltic Finns, and that of the Balts.

Ethnic Balts in the Southern Half of the Eastern Baltic

Written sources reveal that the ethnic Balts fell into several subgroups clearly distinguishable by archaeological material. Some of these groups represented inland people who shall be described here only fleetingly. Coastal areas along the Baltic were home to the Couronians who merited frequent mention in some Nordic sources, whilst being virtually overlooked in others. It is mostly Danish and German sources where we hear talk of inhabitants of *Samland* or *Semland*, in all probability ethnic Balts populating land in what later became Prussia, partly what is the present-day Kaliningrad region of the Russian Federation and partly in northeastern Poland today. Sure enough, the German name for the Sambia Peninsula in the Kaliningrad region is *Samland*.

During the Viking Age, the areas inhabited by ethnic Balts were generally characterized by a distinctive, rich, regionally diverse ethnic culture. Scandinavian influence was weak or non-existent, even though it was precisely here, *Samland* and Couronia, where the only Eastern Baltic Scandinavian colonies of Grobiņa and Kaup, respectively, were formed. It seems, however, that the influence of western colonists did not extend much beyond these colonies.

In nearly all regions inhabited by ethnic Balts, archaeologists have found extensive burial grounds with multiple interments. Most of these burials are accompanied by grave goods. The Balts' material culture has been particularly well analysed in relation to areas dominated by inhumation graves containing well-preserved metal artefacts. All these areas are characterized by a multiplicity of hill-forts often surrounded by large settlements. These hill-forts served as political hubs, some of them possibly linked with trade routes. Many of the hill-forts may have functioned as cult centres, especially where two or more of them stood in close proximity to one another.

Of those ethnic Balts who lived inland, the Semgallians had the easiest access to the sea. The Semgallian area, which straddles today's Latvia and Lithuania, centred on the mighty Lielupe River and its many tributaries. These fertile lands were cut off from the sea and the Daugava River by a barren strip of land some twelve to nineteen miles wide and with virtually no human habitation in prehistoric times. The territories south and east of the Semgallian land were home to the rest of the Baltic peoples, due to the fact that the Lielupe River does not flow far inland.

Solid knowledge of Semgallian material culture owes much to the large and archaeologically well-explored cemeteries containing inhumation graves (Fig. 1). Various grave goods, for example certain types of jewellery or weaponry, are characteristic of Semgallians alone, or may be associated with the inhabitants in a few neighbouring areas, like the Latgallians or Zhemaitians. Certain types of artefacts believed to be Semgallian have, however, been found in abundance

Figure 1. Artefacts from a Semgallian male inhumation burial at Podiņi A, eleventh century (National History Museum of Latvia (LVNM) A 10184: 4–9). Photograph by R. Kaniņš. Courtesy of the National History Museum of Latvia.

in Courland, on the Estonian island of Saaremaa, and also at the Daugava estuary where they seem to be rooted in the local culture. These items probably reflect the cultural ties along the Lielupe and the Daugava, and on lands along adjacent shores.

The *Samland* or *Semland* occasionally mentioned in Scandinavian sagas and other written sources is probably identifiable with the coastal areas of latter-day Prussia, as we mentioned above. Semgallia features in the Norse sagas only once, if at all, when Yngvar the Traveller and Prince Onundr forced the local chieftains to resume paying taxes to the king of Sweden (*The Saga of Yngvar the Traveller*, chap. 4). An eleventh-century runic stone and a copper box found in Sigtuna, inland from Stockholm, both carry the toponym *Simkala* which has also been identified as Semgallia (Zilmer 2005, 175–79).

The Latgallian and Selonian lands stretched along the banks of the Daugava, a little less than one hundred kilometres from its estuary. These Baltic peoples seem to have had a distinct material culture which has been revealed through numerous inhumation cemeteries containing rich grave goods. However, they lived too far from the Baltic Sea to have received any significant influence from Scandinavia; nor do they get any mention in the Nordic sources either. Nonetheless, there can be no doubt that Latgallians in particular played a crucial role in the Daugava trade with the Russian principalities and Byzantium further south.

Couronia as Meeting-Place of Different Cultures

Researchers' ideas of what exactly comprises Couronia (or *Kurland / Courland* in much historical literature) differ in different countries. Lithuanian archaeologists commonly identify Couronia as the land along the present-day Lithuanian shore plus a chunk of Latvia's coast immediately north. For Latvian, Estonian, and Finnish archaeologists, on the other hand, Couronia is first and foremost represented by the Kurzeme peninsula and the coastal area south of it (see Map 1 above). Indeed, the Latvian *Kurzeme* literally means Cour-Land, as do the Estonian *Kuramaa* and the Finnish *Kuurinmaa*. We should perhaps note the name Kuresaar (Cour-Island), the old name for Estonia's largest island, Saaremaa, which is located right across the Kurzeme peninsula. Archaeologically the Iron Age culture of Saaremaa bore in many respects greater resemblance to Couronia than it did to the main part of mainland Estonia.

The *Kurlanders*, or *Kuri* named in written sources, are believed to be ethnic Balts, probably not the least because their historical area of habitation today falls under Latvia and Lithuania. Latvian archaeologists do admit, however, that even during the Viking Age northern Couronia was inhabited by Baltic Finns, and the ethnic Baltic Cours only gradually expanded their area of habitation. One-time inhabitants of the northern part of Couronia are frequently called Couronian Livs by Latvian archaeologists, even in the face of convincing proof of the erroneous nature of the definition, given that the Livonian fishing villages did not make an appearance at the sandy and sparsely populated northern tip of Couronia until the fourteenth century.

The earlier Baltic Finns of Couronia, regularly called *kuralased / kuurilaiset* in Estonian and Finnish archaeological literature, thus represented a different ethnic group altogether, one that later assimilated with the Balts. Today, all that remains is the Tami dialect spoken in western Couronia which has strong Baltic Finnic elements, and several Baltic Finnic place-names found even as far south as today's Lithuania.

Stone graves of a Baltic Finnic-type, albeit still awaiting further examination, have been discovered in the northern part of Couronia. Most Baltic Finnic burials date from the tenth or eleventh centuries and Latvian archaeology occasionally describes the eleventh to fourteenth century inhabitants of the lower and middle reaches of the Venta River as "Couronianized Livs". Finds from inhumation burials in this region are almost identical to items recovered from graves in Saaremaa and the Livic cemeteries, even if inhumation burials were rare among Baltic Finns and occur in just a few areas. Couronia, though, abounds in cremation burials and this is commonly viewed in Latvian archaeology as indicative of Baltic Cours. Indeed, the Late Iron Age finds from cremation burials in central Couronia for the most part emulate designs developed among the Cours and presumably indicate a gradual northward spread of ethnic Baltic settlement. Conspicuously, a large variety of artefacts can be associated simultaneously with the Cours and with Saaremaa and coastal Estonia, an obvious demonstration of the close ties these areas must have maintained over times.

Compared to the northern part of Couronia, the grave sites in the lands of the (Baltic) Cours are much more numerous and far better examined. At the start of the Viking Age, the dominant mode of burial in these regions was inhumation, only to be replaced by predominantly individual cremation burials somewhat later. Most of these burials are characterized by an abundance of grave goods, with jewellery equally plentiful in women's and men's graves (Fig. 2).

Most Scandinavian-type artefacts found in Couronia have been recovered from burial sites in the vicinity of the local Scandinavian colony in Grobiņa and in the areas north

Figure 2. Artefacts from male inhumation grave number 199 at Palanga cemetery, Couronia, second half of the tenth century (Griciuvienė 2009: 1186). Courtesy of the National Museum of Lithuania.

of it. The bulk of these finds are pre-Viking Age or from the early days of the Viking Age proper. In the southern part of Couronia, on the other hand, Scandinavian artefacts were rare.[1]

Thus defined, it is clear that Couronia was home to two ethnic groups, speakers of different linguistic families living without an explicit demarcation line between the communities' areas of settlement. And to all appearances, their differences went far beyond just the language they spoke. As much as we know (admittedly little) about the Baltic and Baltic Finnic mythologies, they represented very dissimilar views of the world. As we will discover later, certain divergences were also evident in the social organization of the Balts and Baltic Finns, in their genus systems, and probably in many other aspects as well.

Extant written sources, however, seem to describe just one variety of Couronian. On the other hand, upon closer study the terms *Kúrland* and *Samland* seem to at least partly overlap. Saxo Grammaticus, the historian (ca. 1160–1220) of the *Deeds of the Danes*, for one, tells how during one of his voyages Ragnar Lodbrok ended up "in the land of Couronians and Sambians" ("in Curorum Semborumque regionem" (from the *Gesta Danorum* of Saxo Grammaticus, bk. 9, chap. 4, §23, hereaf-

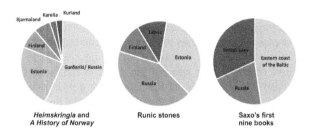

Figure 3. Pie-chart diagrams of modern regions cited in different
written sources. For the first two diagrams, only
areas in the eastern Baltic Sea are depicted.

ter cited in the format 9.4.23). In the past, the term *Samit*
was used to denote the Baltic Finnic inhabitants of Courland.
Going by the name of Kuresaar in earlier times, Saaremaa
is still Samzala, or Sam-Island, in modern Latvian. As one
possible interpretation, *Kúrland* and *Samland* may both have
been used to identify inhabitants of Couronia and Kuresaar/
Samzala who spoke different languages. It is also possible
that "Couronian" initially had a social connotation, much the
same as "Viking" in fact meant just a sea rover. *Kuri* is a Baltic
Finnic word for something wicked, stern, or ill-natured, and
as such quite fitting to describe certain natives of Couronia—
those who engaged in piracy.

Interestingly, written sources diverge considerably in
their coverage of Couronians. The famous Old Norse kings'
saga, *Heimskringla*, hardly mentions Couronia at all, and
the toponym only rarely makes an appearance in the other
Icelandic sagas (Fig. 3). The more or less contemporaneous
Gesta Danorum by Saxo Grammaticus, however, is quite a different matter. Self-avowedly relying on the same sources as
the Icelandic sagas, Saxo is rather chatty about Curonians.
On the other hand, he seems to have never heard of Saaremaa which is probably mentioned in the Icelandic stories
more frequently than any other Eastern Baltic location. Like-

wise, only on a few occasions does Saxo refers to *Estland*. This inevitably leads to a conclusion that although the stories spring from the same sources, the writers have their own preferences when it comes to ethnonyms and toponyms.

Couronia, however, merited a longer description in the Rimbert chronicle that was written down in the ninth century. Also, the Saga of Burnt Njall speaks of a Viking raid on Couronia, probably somewhere near the Venta River. Both narratives are long and relatively detailed and have certainly cemented the image of Couronia as a very important region in Viking Age communication.

The People who Gave their Name to Medieval Livonia

The lower reaches of the Daugava River and the edge of the Gulf of Riga had provided human settlement for millennia. The Daugava fed into the gulf with Couronia to the west on the Baltic, Estonia to the north, and Saaremaa island at the head of the bay. This lower valley and the territories immediately north of it were inhabited by the Livs—a Baltic Finnic people who gave the whole northern Baltic region its medieval name of Livonia. Archaeologically, the Livs are distinguished by burial grounds with numerous individual burials, both inhumations and cremations. Inhumation cemeteries were rather exceptional among the Baltic Finns, and in the Livic tradition probably shows a strong cultural influence exerted by their Baltic neighbours.

Moreover, the Livic burials were characterized by rich grave goods with many types of artefact that bear a striking resemblance to finds from Scandinavia—so much so that, when the first Livic graves were excavated at the end of the nineteenth century, they were interpreted as Scandinavian burial sites. This theory was conditioned by ideas that dominated Latvian archaeology through to the Second World War, which pictured the late prehistoric Baltic Finns as savages culturally inferior to the Balts.[2] When compared against the unique material culture of the Baltic people, the Livic artefacts indeed displayed distinctive Scandinavian influence. However, the comparative similarity of cultures was likewise characteristic of other Baltic Finnic coastal areas: in fact, it is northern Couronia and Saaremaa to which Livic culture had the closest resemblance.

The hill-forts situated in the lower reaches of the Daugava River date from various centuries, yet the oldest Livic burials are dated to the second half of the tenth century and, further north, to the beginning of the eleventh century. This timeline has encouraged theories about the Livs not arriving at the river's lower reaches until the middle of the tenth century. The Livs were believed to have originated from northern Couronia—even though no Baltic Finnic burials from the early Viking Age have been located there. In fact, territories populated by Baltic Finns in Estonia, part of Finland, and northwestern Russia also provide just a few burials, or even none at all, to have been unearthed from the period 650 to 950. So burial patterns shed no light on the pre-Viking settlement of the people known later as Livs.

Several Latvian archaeologists have identified the Semgallians as the pre-Livic inhabitants of the lower Daugava, since a few burials with probably Semgallian items have been found here.[3] Similar artefacts have been recovered from hill-forts; however, there is no trace in their vicinity of the large inhumation cemeteries commonly found in the Semgallians' main area of habitation. The handful of finds discovered so far bear a resemblance to not only Semgallian items but, likewise, to those found in Saaremaa, across the large bay opposite the northern peninsula of Couronia.

Like the Semgallians, the Livs were essentially not coastal dwellers. Their fields reached the sea in just a few places, and even on the northern banks of the Daugava the fields lay more than ten kilometres from the seashore. This might explain why the Icelandic sagas only rarely mention *Lifland*— or perhaps the Livs may have simply been subsumed under the definition of Estonians or Couronians. Mention was more frequently made, for example in *Göngu-Hrólfs Saga* (chap. 28), of the large river *Dýnu* on the *Austrvegr*. This was the waterway that provided access to *Garðaríki*, the area beyond which took the Vikings to the lands of the Rus', Constantinople, and the Arab world beyond.[4] Saxo Grammaticus seems to know a lot more about the purported Livs: *Hellespont* is his name for their territory and the large river running through it.

Baltic Finnic Peoples in the Northern Half of the Eastern Baltic

Estonia today lies at the heart of the Viking Age Baltic Finnic world. It bordered on the other Baltic Finnic peoples to the north, the east, and also to the south. Settlement intermingled with the ethnic Balts, the Latgallians to be more precise, can be hypothesized to have existed only in northeast of modernday Latvia. Extant material culture shows Estonia split into two major cultural spheres: coastal and inland. So-called coastal Estonia consisted of the islands and the western and northwestern regions of mainland Estonia. This was a region supporting a strong maritime culture and characterized by influence from eastern Scandinavia and the southwestern Finland—in contrast to the inland territories and the northeastern coast sharing a cultural milieu shared with the Baltic Finns further east.

Cultural contrasts between inland and coast were also highly visible in Finland where during the Viking Age Baltic Finnic settlement was gradually moving north, towards the Sami people's territories.[5] The densely populated western and southwestern regions of Finland were culturally comparable to eastern Scandinavia; intense relations with Middle Sweden had characterized these regions for centuries, even millennia, before the Viking Age. Communication with Middle Sweden was facilitated by the Åland archipelago where the Viking Age population, judging by their material culture, seems to have been made up of Scandinavians (see *The Viking Age in Åland* in the Further Reading section).

The Viking Age saw Baltic Finns still inhabiting nearly the whole of what is now northwestern Russia. It was a region that saw a massive influx of eastern Slavic peoples—into trading and political centres in particular. The areas around Lake Ladoga and southeast of the Gulf of Finland were widely populated by native Baltic Finnic speakers till a few centuries ago with ethnic Russians concentrated in the major settlements; any Baltic Finnic survivors of Stalin's purges are now a tiny minority of Novgorod, Pskov oblasts, or St. Petersburg.

Throughout the Viking Age and during the eleventh and twelfth centuries, a large part of this Baltic Finnic territory practised collectivist cremation burial in which the remains of the dead were mixed and so became indistinguishable (Mägi 2018, 34–44). This tradition saw the grave goods chopped into pieces before being placed on the pyre and burned. The fragments of various items and cremated bones collected from the pyre were scattered across the burial sites, either deposited between stones or, especially in Finland, into rock crevices, or spread on the ground. In some places, the burial remains were covered with cairns.

The molten fragments from such cremation burials are obviously less attractive than the intact finds recovered from the inhumation graves of the Balts. Even though the artefacts are mostly recognizable from the fragments, this particular custom has inevitably created the deceptive impression that the Baltic Finns' burial grounds—and, consequently, their whole society—were somehow "poorer" than the cemeteries of the ethnic Balts. Nonetheless, in comparison with the latter, the Baltic Finns' burial rites make it impossible for scholars to identify the number of the deceased at a burial site, let alone link the grave goods to specific burials. In all likelihood these were family burial grounds where any demonstration of individuality was consciously avoided. Estonian and Finnish researchers have come up with a theory that these burials were reserved exclusively for members of the ruling families whereas the rest of the dead were buried in a way that left no archaeological trace.

This demonstration of collectivist values through burial rites, in all likelihood primarily clan- or family-based ones, which saw the bones of the departed mixed, probably indicates a corporate mode of power. Such societies were neither egalitarian nor democratic, and power was exercised by a few elite families, usually through various assemblages which may have overlapped with each other, or may have been based on different social arenas, for instance military affairs or clan structures (Mägi 2018, 41–44).

The burials in Estonia, northwestern Russia, and part of Finland often did not become "visible" until the second half of the tenth century, as we showed above. Only a few burial sites from the period 650–950, some clusters of items recovered from stone graves and other locations, are known from these regions. The period may have witnessed the custom of bringing the cremated remains of the departed to family burial sites, however, but we cannot identify these burials due to the lack of grave goods. On the other hand, the centuries-long "void" of grave finds have produced a wide array of offerings and hoards, and in Estonia we also see hill-fort and settlement complexes. In this way we can demonstrate continued habitation of the Baltic Finnic territories, albeit their concept of the afterworld may not have generated actual graves or (metal) grave goods that have been preserved for us.

However, there was one big exception in the Baltic Finnic burial tradition that we have described—the Eura neighbourhood in western Finland. This relatively small area has at least three cemeteries with numerous inhumation burials. These burial sites had foundations laid in the sixth century and stayed in use through the eighth and ninth centuries (a period that was quite "empty" elsewhere), all the way through to the twelfth century (Lehtosalo-Hilander, *Luistari III*). Some of the Eura burials have yielded a plethora of weapons and jewellery and so they are helpful in dating items found elsewhere as stray finds or recovered from otherwise structureless stone graves. The Luistari and Köyliö cemeteries in particular, and the theories they have helped to shape, are often used in discussions concerning not just the Finnish, but also the Estonian Viking Age—despite them being exceptions to the rule.

The material cultures of Viking Age and eleventh–twelfth century Finnish and Estonian coastal areas are characteristic because many types of artefact are identical to those used in eastern Scandinavia. This is particularly evident in items associated with warriors: weaponry, certain jewellery, and other accessories. The local culture also adopted Germanic animal-style ornaments by at least the eighth century (Mägi 2018, 238–40).

Estonia and Finland as well as the other Baltic Finnic regions are mentioned in the Icelandic sagas quite often, albeit briefly (Map 2). Estonia, the Livic lands, Couronia in Latvia, and the coastal region of today's northwestern Russia were all covered by the concept of *Austrvegr* (literally, the Eastern Way) which denoted both the route to the east and the lands in the east. Finland merits frequent mention in relation to familial ties—it seems that the *Finns* were related through marriages to *Garðaríki* as well as to the Yngling dynasty of Sweden.

> Vanlandi was the name of Sveigthir's son who succeeded him and ruled over the Uppsala crown goods. He was a great warrior and fared far and wide from country to country. He accepted an invitation to pass the winter in Finland with Snæ the Old, and there he married his daughter Drífa. But in the spring he departed, leaving Drífa behind. He promised to return after three years, but did not within ten years. Then Drífa sent for Huld, a sorceress, and sent Vísbur, her son by Vanlandi, to Sweden (*The Saga of the Ynglings*, chap. 13).

Visbur became the next king in Uppsala. Only a few reigns later Finland was attacked by the Swedes again.

> One summer King Agni proceeded to Finland with his fleet, landing and harrying there. The Finns collected a great force to oppose him. The name of their leader was Frosti. A great battle ensued, and King Agni was victorious. Frosti and a great many others fell there. King Agni harried far and wide in Finland, subjecting it and making enormous booty. He took Skjálf, Frosti's daughter, prisoner and carried her away together with Logi, her brother. King Agni proceeded to marry Skjálf. She prayed the king to make a funeral feast for her father. So he invited many men of note and celebrated a great feast (*The Saga of the Ynglings*, chap. 19).

Map 2. Selected place-names from Norse sagas and
their presumed locations in the early Viking Age
(the areas denoted of Svearíki and Garðaríki are
marked by different hatching).

During the feast Skjálf managed to hang king Agni with his
own golden chain but escaped together with her men.

At times it is unclear whether the *Finns* in this context
stand for Finns proper or the Sami people but at any rate they
are, more often than not, associated with sorcery. In addition,
references are made to certain place-names in Finland, for
example *Kvenland* (Häme?) or *Bálagarðssíða* (the southwestern areas?).

Such stories are mostly found in the so-called legendary sagas that are set in an undetermined past and are of

little value in terms of authenticity. Also, the first saga of *Heimskringla*, the so-called Ynglinga Saga, has been compared to these legendary sagas. Legendary sagas are often set on the eastern shores of the Baltic Sea, or even farther east, in *Bjarmaland*, and the events they describe may refer to the confusing times of the pre-Viking Age and the first half of the Viking Age, when the Scandinavians were still busy trying to establish themselves in *Austrvegr*.

The Ynglinga Saga, its basic source *Ynglingatal*, and some other legendary sagas occasionally refer to raids to *Austrvegr* and, more specifically, to *Estland*, modern Estonia. A similar picture is painted in *A History of Norway*. These attacks were not solely instigated by the Scandinavians, being often inspired by the forays of *Austrvegr* men into the realms of the Swedish kings. As far as Estonia is concerned, the sagas—as we would expect—refer to the coastal areas, Saaremaa (*Eysýsla*) in particular, and the rest of coastal Estonia (*Aðalsýsla*) going under the collective name *Sýslar* (see Map 2 above).[6]

The sagas covering the tenth and eleventh centuries mention *Rafala* (near the modern city of Tallinn), Estonian Vikings, the captivity of King Olaf Trygvasson in Estonia, and several raids.[7] The stories telling of earlier periods most probably classify inland Estonia and the northeastern part of the country, or *Virland* (modern Virumaa) under *Garðaríki*. This is strongly implied by the multiple descriptions of Viking raids since they could not have possibly taken place in the inland regions of contemporary Russia. During the Viking Age the "Chuds", who the Russian chronicles say played a major role in the emergence of the earliest state, can probably be identified as inhabitants of inland Estonia and *Virland*—as opposed to the *Sosol'* (from the toponym *Sýslar*), or inhabitants of coastal Estonia.

The mostly eleventh-century runic stones found in Middle Sweden name the eastern territories about twice as often as they mention the western areas (see Fig. 3 above). Of all these stones, eleven refer to one or another location in *Garðaríki*, nine to places in Estonia, three to Finland, and the final three to Latvia, the Daugava estuary, and northern Couronia (Zilmer 2005). This seems to agree with the information derived from the sagas and archaeological material about the relative importance of certain Eastern Baltic locations in maintaining the overseas links to Scandinavia.

Cultural Communication between the Eastern Baltic and Scandinavia

The information gleaned from the archaeological evidence available to us points to two different modes of communication between the Eastern Baltic and Scandinavia (Map 3). The results are perhaps unexpected. Scandinavian influence in these territories seems to manifest itself in a slightly surprising way. First, the only Scandinavian colonies are known in the ethnic Balts' territories in the southern half of the Eastern Baltic, but their cultural influence is restricted to those settlements and probably no further than a few dozen miles around the colonies. Thus, Scandinavians seem to have had no meaningful impact on the culture of the ethnic Balts there.

The situation seems to have been the opposite in the Baltic Finnic coastal areas of Estonia, Finland, and Latvia which adopted a multitude of Scandinavian attributes—from types of artefact and ornament to certain grave styles—and they made them their own. Yet as far as is known, these coastal areas which displayed particularly strong cultural influence hosted no Scandinavian colonies at all (see the crosshatched section of Map 3).

The phenomenon where certain areas accommodate foreign colonies which fail to have any significant cultural impact on the locals has been called "middle ground colonialism" (Gosden 2004, 26–32). In this situation both the colonists and the natives feel that they are in control. There is no acculturation, and while the newcomers and the local residents may be somewhat dependent on each other, their contacts may be brief and not too productive. Middle ground colonialism is also relatively short-lived from the historical point of view— the settlers will either assimilate, return to their homeland, or get killed.

Map 3. Different modes of cultural communication.
Crosshatching denotes shared cultural milieux for warriors,
simple hatching the area of middle-ground colonialism
with distinct Scandinavian colonies.

It is this sort of middle ground colonialism that seems to have existed in the Baltic Sea coastal areas inhabited by the ethnic Balts. Typically, each of these colonies probably constituted a socially compact community composed of individuals of both sexes, of various ages, and at various status levels, as evidenced by the graves of Scandinavian men and women excavated at burial sites near Grobiņa and Kaup. Similarly, most of the Viking Age Scandinavian colonies that thrived within what is today Russia without their cultural impact extending beyond the specific location could be categorized as middle ground colonialism. The only exception in this respect is the southern shore of Lake Ladoga which has yielded archaeological material matching the other Baltic Finnic coastal areas.

Examples where a particular culture seems to be strongly influenced by a neighbouring nation without the presence of any colonies, is defined by Gosden as "colonialism within a shared cultural milieu" (*Archaeology of Colonialism*, 26, 39–81). This phenomenon is usually limited to a single sector of the local society, like wealthier tradesmen or elite warriors, the more mobile members of the community who are simultaneously more susceptible to foreign influences. Such an elite group, or part thereof, would want to stand out from their own community by adopting certain foreign accessories, clothing, or behaviour, sometimes also their language—all this to emphasize their position and status while simultaneously maintaining ties to their native society. This system is characterized by close personal contacts with the elites of their adopted culture, multilingualism, and the hybrid nature of the cultures.

The discourse of shared cultural milieux has been dubbed "colonialism without colonies" because this type of cultural behaviour does not envisage, require, and indeed does not even enable, the emergence of settlements from the outside culture. Certain spatial mobility does occur, though, but almost exclusively restricted to the individuals active in the common cultural sphere, like the previously mentioned elite warriors and traders. This pattern does not necessarily mean that items depicting this common cultural sphere are imported from the core regions. On the contrary, the adopted styles will often be produced locally, and with local variations.

During the pre-Viking and Viking Age, such a shared cultural milieu is what we find in several coastal areas inhabited by the Baltic Finns. Items recovered here from female graves predominantly represent local types, while the artefacts associated with warriors bear a striking resemblance to analogous finds from eastern Sweden. This shared cultural milieu of warriors became highly visible in archaeological evidence from the second half of the tenth century onwards when the Baltic Finnic burials begin to show a significant increase in the number of grave goods across all their territories.

Summing up, it is fair to say that by the end of the Viking Age at the latest, warriors from the Baltic Finnic coastal areas were archaeologically indistinguishable from warriors of Gotland or Middle Sweden. However, it is important to remember that in all these territories there were notable differences between the material cultures of inland and coastal areas. Scandinavian influence was much weaker in inland areas and, by and large, communicated through contacts with the Scandinavian colonies established in what is today Russia.

Notes

[1] Audrone Bliujienė, "Role of the Curonians in the Eastern Baltic Area: The Transition Process from the Late Migration Period into the Early Viking Age (Cultural Aspects)," in *Transformatio Mundi*, ed. Bertašius [see Further Reading], 183-93.

[2] Andris Šnē, "Social Structures of Livonian Society in the Late Iron Age (10th-Early 13th Century)," in *Arkeologi över gränser. Möten mellan lettisk och svensk arkeologi,* ed. Ola Jensen, Håkan Karlsson, and Armands Vijups (Göteborg: Göteborgs Universitet, 1997), 183-207.

[3] Arnis Radiņš, "Lower Daugava Area in the 1st to 11th Century. Ethnic, Economic, Social and Political Change—on the Question of Activity along Daugava Waterway," in *Transformatio Mundi*, ed. Bertašius 81-92.

[4] *Austrvegr* (the "Eastern Way") denoted both the route to the east and the coastal areas east of the Baltic Sea. *Garðaríki* is normally translated as Russia, but its exact meaning changed over time. Both terms are discussed later in this volume.

[5] Joonas Ahola and Frog, "Approaching the Viking Age in Finland. An Intoduction," in *Fibula, Fabula, Fact*, 21-84.

[6] *The Saga of the Ynglings*, chaps. 32, 33; *Ynglingatal*, chap. 25; *A History of Norway*, chap. 13:22-24.

[7] *The Story of Burnt Njal*, chap. 30; *A History of Norway*, chap. 23; *The Saga of Óláf Tryggvason*, chap. 90; *Saint Óláf's Saga*, chap. 8.

Chapter 2

Eastbound Routes Gain Momentum

Even though the Viking Age is generally taken to cover the period 800 to 1000/1050, the features that came to characterize this era first emerged many centuries earlier. In the fifth and sixth centuries of our era, the whole of Northern Europe experienced a surge in military activity across societies, a rise in weapon burials, and growing hierarchy in social structures. Long-distance trade boomed, and the Eastern Baltic was no exception in this respect. In fifth- and sixth-century Finland and Estonia, imports from the lands of eastern Finno–Ugric speakers and Scandinavia showed a remarkable increase (Fig. 4 and Fig. 5).

Contacts across the Baltic Sea were certainly facilitated by the introduction of sail technology, instead of or to supplement rowing. Despite speculation that sails may have been used in the Baltic much earlier, there is no evidence of sailing boats before the seventh century. Anyway, it is at about that time that sailing across the open sea appears to have become commonplace. In archaeology it is accompanied by a rapid Scandinavianization of several coastal areas in the Eastern Baltic.

The pre-Viking centuries saw not just the intensification of overseas contacts along the Baltic shoreline, but also increasingly important trade routes to faraway regions, like the Volga and Kama River basins. Most of these routes crossed the Eastern Baltic or followed its coast.

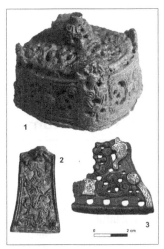

Figure 4. Examples of Viking Age Scandinavian jewellery found in Estonia. 1: Kasari (in private possession), 2: Linnakse (Archive of Archaeological Research Collections, Tallinn University (TLU AI) 6961: 115), 3: Paatsa (Estonian History Museum (AM) A 136: 1). Photographs by I. Jets.

Figure 5. Examples of Viking Age ornaments from coastal Estonia. 1 and 2: Viidumäe (private possession), 3: Karja (TLU AI K 77: 6), 4: Mõisaküla (TLU AI 2602: 8), 5: Iru (TLU AI 4051: 7), 6: Saaremaa (TLU AI K 83: 22). Photographs by M. Mägi and I. Jets.

Routes and Stopping Places

There is a broad consensus among researchers that early prehistoric travellers preferred waterways to overland routes whenever and wherever possible. Especially in forested areas the maintenance of paths was difficult and they became almost impassable in spring and autumn. The sprawling wetlands, especially in the northern half of the Eastern Baltic, complicated travelling in summer yet provided a good base for winter roads during the frozen period. Seasonality of communication networks was a distinctive feature of the whole of Northern Europe.

Rivers, on the other hand, were navigable nearly all the year round: in summer by boats, and in winter by sledges. During the spring floods pushed water levels in the rivers of the northeastern coast of the Baltic Sea significantly higher for weeks, so even otherwise barely passable waterways could be travelled. We need to remember too that, while the land mass is rising in the northern half of the Eastern Baltic (Estonia and Finland) it is sinking in present-day northwestern Russia. Movements of the land mass influence not only coastal lines, but also inland areas, for instance wetlands, that are often sources for rivers. Another factor that strongly influences the discharge of water in rivers are changes to drainage patterns, a more modern feature. As a result of these various factors, compared to the Viking Age, rivers are now considerably smaller in Estonia, but larger in Russia. In Finland land-mass rises have been even more pronounced, resulting in dramatic changes in the landscape when compared to a thousand years ago. In Latvia and Lithuania, on the other hand, the changes are minimal and primarily affect coastal areas.

Viking Age ships probably sailed via waterways to anywhere they had access. However, by that time certain routes, with harbours along the way, had been well mapped and were used intensively, especially by cargo ships and voyagers with peaceful intentions. In terms of stopping places, most crews preferred to find a landing place, a safe harbour for the night from where they could replenish provisions or, if necessary, wait for more favourable weather before resuming their journey.

Most Viking ships were small and light enough to be dragged ashore. On the other hand, local residents could quite legitimately attack the vessels that came ashore at natural landing places outside the harbour sites. The seafarers' security thus primarily depended on the number of warriors on board, and the ships, cargo boats in particular, always preferred to make berth at a recognized harbour.

Beside topographical factors—natural features offering easy access—international trade routes clearly depended on the existence of a good sequence of harbours. To be able to supply visiting crews with food and other essentials Iron Age harbours needed to have good arable lands nearby. Unavailability or shortage of supplies in the neighbourhood would cause serious problems, especially if a ship—or several ships—were suddenly forced to winter over. A small village or perhaps just a handful of farms would fall under considerable pressure when asked to supply provisions, particularly so at times of distress.

Not even the heavily indented coasts of Estonia and Finland had extensive arable lands stretching all the way to the sea in all places. A proper harbour site was also expected to have a shelving shore and offer shelter from the winds, and a trading place required access to the hinterland, which could be provided by a river. Spurred by the growing eastern trade, harbours seem to have sprung up on the Eastern Baltic shores wherever these conditions were met. Ships needed safe landing places while harbours provided income for the locals.

The intensity of international trade, and consequently the use of trade routes, depended on various factors, like destinations and political circumstances. The final centuries before the Viking period witnessed a boom in two routes traversing the Eastern Baltic: the Eastern Way to the Volga River basin and further south, what the sagas called the *Austrvegr*; and the Amber Way running along the Vistula and the Danube to Southern Europe, the Mediterranean, and to Byzantium (Map 4).

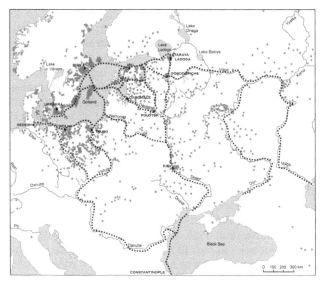

Map 4. Viking Age eastbound trade routes and key
waterways and trade centres. Dots mark finds of dirhams.

The First Scandinavian Colony on the Eastern Coast of the Baltic

The Couronian coastline is long and straight and short of
natural landing places. The beach has extensive sand dunes
that are constantly changing and the landscape can be transformed beyond recognition with one big storm. In the Viking
Age, a small lagoon at the estuary of the small Ālande River
now running through modern-day Latvia a few miles from
the Lithuanian border formed a suitable landing place; the
lagoon offered shelter from the winds. Today it is a beach
lake on the outskirts of the town of Liepāja. Grobiņa, the only
Scandinavian colony known from the Baltics, now lies a few
miles inland.

Unfortunately, Grobiņa had no large river providing access
inland, and the settlement is nowhere near any major eastern

routes—meaning that the colony probably had nothing to do with trade targeted at the eastern markets. However, ships sailing from Middle Sweden or Gotland straight across the Baltic and aiming for the Vistula estuary in its southeastern corner (see Map 4), would find that the lagoon by Grobiņa was the best natural landing place in Couronia. Good arable lands and a fairly dense local population would have provided favourable conditions for the emergence of an international harbour there.

However, no international trading post is known from Grobiņa. We know instead of a hill-fort with an extensive settlement layer located within the modern town of Grobiņa. While archaeologically almost unexcavated, the complex is believed to have grown and developed over a long period of time. The many burial grounds excavated in the neighbourhood have yielded mostly local finds. As a striking exception, however, a few cemeteries appear to have belonged to eastern Scandinavians—as evidenced by grave goods—from either Middle Sweden or Gotland. These burial grounds have been dated to the period from the seventh to early or mid-ninth centuries, that is, the period predating the Viking Age.

The Scandinavian cemeteries of Grobiņa contain burials of both men and women that can be clearly distinguished from the local population by the specific artefacts deposited in their graves. As in death, so in life they are likely to have formed a separate community, wearing clothes and jewellery different from local customs, and speaking a different language. Theirs must have been a typical socially complex colony comprising individuals of different statuses, and their families. The exact location of the colony is unknown but it must have been somewhere close. Small-scale archaeological excavations conducted on the hill-fort indicate a typical local fortification originating precisely from the period between the ninth and thirteenth centuries, namely the period post-dating the abandonment of the Scandinavian colony.[8]

Other finds from various locations in Couronia, especially those within a few dozen miles of Grobiņa, similarly point to the pre-Viking centuries, or at the very early stages of the

Viking Age. Around this time the region was home to the clearly distinct culture of the indigenous Cours which survived beyond the ninth century. Researchers agree that interaction between the Grobiņa Scandinavians and the locals was insignificant or nearly non-existent (see Virse and Ritums, "The Grobiņa Complex of Dwelling Locations and Burial Sites"). In fact, there is no evidence either for the assimilation of the Grobiņa colonists—from the first half of the ninth century onwards, Scandinavian graves disappear from these cemeteries altogether, making this a typical example of middle ground colonialism where individual colonies of foreigners have no impact on the local culture, and suddenly just cease to exist.

Swedes in the Land of Cori

The Grobiņa colony deserves special mention because its final decades are described in one of the very few Viking Age sources that touch upon the Eastern Baltic—Rimbert's *Vita Ansgari*, or the life of Bishop Ansgar, written in Hamburg–Bremen in the ninth century. The story tells of the attempts of Danes and Swedes to subdue the *Cori* people (probably Couronians). In the 840s the Danes had purportedly tried to subjugate the territories in Couronia that had earlier been under the dominion of the Swedes, but they were badly defeated. The raid of King Olaf on the *Cori* hill-forts of *Seeburg* and *Aputra* in 854 is described by Bishop Rimbert as a roaring success.

> For a certain people named *Cori* had in former time been in subjection to the Swedes, but had a long while since rebelled and refused to be in subjection. The Danes, being aware of this, at the time when the bishop had come into Swedish territory [that is, in the 840s], collected a large number of ships, and proceeded to this country, eager to seize their goods and to subdue them again. Their kingdom contained five towns. When the inhabitants knew of their coming they gathered together and began to resist manfully and to defend their property. Having obtained the victory, they massacred half the Danes and plundered their ships, obtaining from them gold and silver and much spoil.

On hearing this, King Olaf and the Swedes, who wished to win for themselves the reputation that they could do what the Danes had not done, and because this people had formerly been subject to them, collected an immense army and proceeded to these parts. In the first instance they came to a town in their kingdom called *Seeburg*. This town, which contained seven thousand fighting men, they ravaged and despoiled and burnt. They left it with strengthened hopes and, having sent away their ships, set out on a five days journey and hastened with savage intent to another of their towns called *Aputra* in which there were fifteen thousand fighting men. When they reached it, these were shut up in the town, and whilst the one party vigorously attacked the town from outside, the other party defended it from within. In this way eight days went by with the result that, though they fought and waged war from morning till night, and many fell on both sides, neither side obtained the victory (*Rimbert's Chronicle*, chap. 30).

According to the chronicler, the conquest of *Aputra* was successful because the still heathen Swedes turned to the Christian God for help—the whole narrative is in fact a laud to the superiority of Christianity. *Seeburg* is usually identified as Grobiņa, whereas *Aputra* is widely believed to be the hill-fort of Apuolė in modern Lithuania. Other locations on the Couronian coast have been proposed as identifiable with *Seeburg* and *Aputra*, but none of them match the description in the chronicle equally well (Mägi 2018, 246–49).

Rimbert's claims in *Vita Ansgari* about the size of the Couronian hill-forts are obviously exaggerated; in fact, archaeological evidence contradicts the narrative too. Regarding the Grobiņa hill-fort it seems (from grave goods that have been recovered) that burials in the nearby Scandinavian cemetery ceased a few decades before the events described here. Following excavations at the Apuolė hill-fort early in the twentieth century the finds were initially interpreted as proof of a second Scandinavian colony in Couronia,[9] but that theory has since been dismissed. Several types of artefact, including arrowheads, previously identified as exclusively Scandinavian, have now been established as having been more widespread, and do not necessarily indicate the presence of Scandinavians.

Recent years have seen intense discussions about why a group of seventh-century eastern Scandinavians should resettle on the coast of Couronia. Grobiṇa has been, by different scholars, perceived in turn as a military outpost of Scandinavians, a trading centre, or an agrarian colony. The latter seems unlikely, however, considering the density of the indigenous population in the neighbourhood—even though it is plausible that at least some of the colonists could have been engaged in agricultural activities. Domestic agriculture was, after all, the main source of food and the colonists could not have survived without producing some for themselves.

In my opinion, the likeliest reason for the foundation of a Scandinavian colony on that exact spot was trade, especially seeing as Grobiṇa is the most suitable natural landing place on the so-called Amber Way. This trade route from the Couronian coast to the Vistula was in use long before the Viking Age and in its northern leg must have relied heavily on a network of groups speaking the Baltic languages. Towards the end of the eighth century another, by now thoroughly excavated, trading post called Truso sprang up on the Amber Way. True, its choice of location was probably inspired by traffic along the southern coast of the Baltic Sea mainly. The Amber Way can be associated with yet another, hypothetically Scandinavian colony known from the same neighbourhood: Kaup in the present-day Kaliningrad district. The oldest Scandinavian burials there are dated to the middle of the ninth century, or around the period when the Grobiṇa colony ceased to exist.

At any rate, it can be said that by the mid-ninth century, inhabitants of eastern Sweden seem to have lost interest in the historical Amber Way along the Vistula. Not only was the Grobiṇa colony abandoned in Courland, but from that point onwards, Scandinavian finds become very rare in the area in general. The dearth of coin finds in Courland is also indicative of the region's rather insignificant role during the second half of the ninth century and in the expanding eastern trade of the tenth century.

Written Sources about the Northern Half of the Eastern Baltic in the Early Viking Age

While Rimbert dwells on the land of the *Cori* rather extensively, Couronia is only rarely named in Icelandic sagas. Of course, these sagas were written down far later, often as late as the thirteenth and fourteenth centuries, and toponyms inevitably undergo mutation in oral tradition. However, whereas Couronia is never mentioned in the ninth-century *Ynglingatal*, the skaldic poetic text that underlies the prose Ynglinga Saga, it is a much more frequent presence in Danish sources, as can be seen later in this study.

Opinions differ as to whether and to what extent the sagas are helpful in reconstructing history. Of the various sorts of sagas some, like the so-called kings' sagas, are recognized to be historically more valuable than others. The least trustworthy are the so-called legendary sagas which are more like fairy tales set in an indeterminable past. For all that, it is precisely the legendary sagas where the narrative is often set in the Eastern Baltic, in *Garðaríki*, or even farther east, in *Bjarmaland*, reflecting the situation more or less like it may have been imagined in the seventh to ninth centuries. This was the period when the Scandinavians were still trying to establish themselves on the *Austrvegr*. *Garðaríki* was a frequent target of Viking raids, and known for its many "kings" replacing one another in rapid succession.

In my opinion, the snippets of information on the Eastern Baltic that can be gleaned from the sagas should not be dismissed out of hand though, obviously, these tales should be treated exactly like the sort of source material they are. The stories initially passed on by word of mouth probably contain elements of truth—however, the narratives built around them have been heavily modified by the many storytellers and scribes adding their personal angles or substituting places and protagonists. In most cases the "original" narrative is long lost; however, the existence of a certain core anchored in reality (events that may have taken place in the past, albeit at different times and involving different individuals) cannot be ruled out.

The sagas, especially legendary sagas, make frequent, although brief, mention of the northern areas of the Eastern Baltic (see Map 2 above). The *Austrvegr* in the sense of not just the eastern route but also eastern lands seem to be roughly identical to the territory that was at that time populated by the Baltic Finns. Also, the *Garðaríki* of the legendary sagas is identifiable with not so much Kievan Rus' (as it was from the mid-tenth century onwards) as vaguely with its northern part, or broadly speaking, territories of the later principalities of Novgorod, Pskov, and maybe also Polotsk.

The terms *Austrvegr* and *Garðaríki* seem to overlap on occasions, yet on other occasions seem to imply separate areas. At any rate, *Garðaríki* could be accessed through *Austrvegr*, clearly a region dominated by maritime culture. Considering the topographical descriptions, *Austrvegr* mainly comprised modern-day Estonia and Latvia, as becomes evident from the sagas that now and again specify the locations in *Austrvegr* targeted by the Viking raids. Quite often their destination is either *Estland*, *Eysýsla* (Saaremaa or the Estonian islands generally), or sometimes *Aðalsýsla* (coastal areas of northwestern and western Estonia).

The sagas telling of more ancient times seem to describe *Garðaríki* as a region with a maritime culture, a place regularly attacked by the Scandinavian Vikings. This would scarcely have been possible in the principalities of Kievan Rus': these were mostly landlocked and accessible by rivers only. As we have seen, rivers in this part of Russia used to be much smaller and contained plenty of impassable rapids and waterfalls, so boats had to be dragged ashore or portaged. The coast of the Gulf of Finland between modern-day Estonia and St. Petersburg was a marshy area, sparsely populated, and lacking decent farmland, which means frequent raids to this region would not made little sense. Furthermore, there is no evidence in Russian chronicles of any seafaring or maritime activity worth the name. It was not until modern times that Russia became a maritime power on the Baltic Sea.

There is good reason to believe that the sagas' vaguely defined *Garðaríki* initially comprised the densely populated and fertile lands on Estonia's northeastern coast and further inland (Mägi 2018, 158–65). On the other hand, certain stories seem to imply that *Garðaríki* may have incorporated the areas, or at least parts of them, along the Daugava River in modern-day Latvia. The situation changed at the end of the tenth century with the consolidation of power in the principalities of Kievan Rus', when the local elite became Slavicized and the inhabitants of the present-day Estonia went from allies to enemies almost overnight.

The Beginning of the Viking Expeditions

The Ynglinga Saga lists the legendary kings who, over an undefined period, ruled *Svearíki*, or Middle Sweden. Judging by the context, the period is pre- and early-Viking. It also appears that several of the kings married Finnish women (see the first chapter of this book), and in one case presumably a Couronian woman.[10] Estonia is named in these tales mostly in the context of raids from both sides.

> After that Sweden was ruled by Yngvar, the son of King Eystein. He was a great man of war and frequently on board his warships, because before his time there had been many incursions made in Sweden, both by Danes and hordes from *Austrvegr*. King Yngvar concluded a peace with the Danes, and then took to harrying in *Austrvegr*. One summer he summoned his fleet and proceeded to *Eistland* where he harried at a place called *at Steini*. Then the men of *Eistland* came upon him with a great host, and there was a battle. The army of the country was so strong that the Swedes were unable to withstand them. King Yngvar was slain then, and his host fled. He is buried in a mound there, close by the sea, in *Aðalsýsla*. After this defeat the Swedes returned home (*The Saga of the Ynglings*, chap. 32).

The place called *at Steini* which appears to be located somewhere in the east, is mentioned in the same saga in another context, in relation to King Sveigthir (see Mägi 2018, 178–79).

> Sveigthir set out again to look for God Home. In the eastern part of *Svíþjóð* [Swedish dominion] there is a large estate,

called *at Steini*. There stands a boulder as big as a large house. In the evening, after sunset, when Sveigthir went from the feast to his sleeping quarters he saw that a dwarf was sitting by the boulder. Sveigthir and his men were very drunk and ran toward the boulder. The dwarf stood in the doorway (of the rock) and called to Sveigthir, inviting him to enter in if he would see Óthin. Sveigthir ran in, and the rock at once closed after him, and he never came out again (*The Saga of the Ynglings*, chap. 12).

Supposing there is some truth in the place-names and the presence of a conspicuously large boulder, we might conjecture that the events may have taken place in the vicinity of today's Tallinn. Compared to the rest of Northern Europe, Estonia is exceptionally rich in boulders while only a few of them are located in close proximity of suitable harbours and extensive cultivated fields that may have invited plundering raids.

According to the Ynglinga Saga, King Yngvar's son Onund mounted a successful revenge expedition.

Onund was the name of the son of Yngvar, who succeeded him. In his days, good peace prevailed in *Svíþjóð* (Sweden), and he became very wealthy in chattels. King Onund proceeded with his host to *Eistland* to avenge his father. He landed, and harried far and wide and made great booty. In the fall he returned to Sweden. In his days there was great prosperity/fruitful seasons in Sweden (*The Saga of the Ynglings*, chap. 33).

In fact, it is plausible that raids like this were far from rare and originated from both the western and eastern shores of the Baltic Sea. After all, Yngvar's expedition described in the saga was retaliation for attacks on the coast of *Svearíki* committed by men from the east.

Apart from the Icelandic sagas, narratives set in the pre-Viking period and the early days of the Viking Age are brought to us by the Danish writer, Saxo Grammaticus. A contemporary of Snorri Sturluson who penned *Heimskringla*, Saxo wrote at the turn of the twelfth and thirteenth centuries. He has admitted using stories collected in Iceland, and indeed, several of his accounts are reminiscent of tales featured in other sagas, even with the mythical kings of Denmark as protagonists. The biggest difference concerning the Eastern Baltic between his books and the Icelandic sagas is Saxo's use of toponyms.

Several of Saxo's narratives were inspired by old stories that in all likelihood often described events on the Eastern Baltic coasts. Saxo wrote in Latin, translating all the names he found in the oral accounts. In doing this he probably relied on the political circumstances and knowledge prevalent in his own day. It seems that both *Garðaríki* and *Austrvegr* are translated as *Ruthenia*, or Russia. At any rate, in Saxo's texts *Ruthenia* is a territory with a strong maritime culture and somewhat similar to, yet clearly distinct from, his own Scandinavia. As we mentioned earlier, *Ruthenia* (in the sense of the latter Russia) could not possibly be a region with a strong maritime culture, not least for topographical reasons.

Indeed, Saxo's book occasionally appears to imply that *Ruthenia* is home to both *Curlandia* and *Hellespont* (the Daugava River; Saxo Grammaticus, 6.5.9, 8.8.9, and 9.4.32). Surprisingly, Saxo seems to be quite oblivious of places like *Eysýsla* or *Aðalsýsla* which often figure in the Icelandic sagas, and the toponym *Esthonia* only rarely makes an appearance. It is possible that in Saxo's interpretation these places represented just one part of *Ruthenia*. On the other hand, Couronia and the Couronians, together with *Samland* (probably later Prussia), are brought up with striking frequency.

Anyway, judging by Saxo's mythical stories, the earliest Norse legendary kings seem to have been particularly active in the east. And again, it appears that the expeditions were not one-directional or carried out by Scandinavians alone. "At that time Reth, a *Ruthenian* pirate, was devastating our homeland with barbarous pillage and violence," Saxo writes to justify the Danes' Viking raids to eastern territories (Saxo Grammaticus, 7.9.7; see also 2.1.6). Reth is by no means the only sea lord of *Ruthenia* encountered in Saxo's texts. Returning from a raid on Couronia, Frotho King of Denmark had a brush at sea with the "Russian" (*Ruthenae*) chieftain Tranno, and later attacked several hill-forts in *Ruthenia* to which he obviously must have had access by ship (Saxo Grammaticus, 2.1.4–6 and 7–9). It makes sense to assume that these hill-forts were located on the Estonian coast, or perhaps along the lower reaches of the Daugava, and not deep inland in Kievan Rus' where access by river would have been very complicated indeed (Mägi 2018, 158–65).

Hill-Forts along Austrvegr

As we saw in the opening chapter, Baltic Finnic funerary rituals did not involve any grave goods at this period, which makes archaeology difficult for the northern half of the Eastern Baltic Fortunately, we also saw that, compared to Scandinavia, the Baltics and northwestern Russia were exceptionally rich in hill-forts, and most of these were in intensive use—this could possibly be the etymology behind the name *Garðaríki* ("State of Towns / Strongholds"). Indeed, the majority of these wooden fortresses strongly resembled the Scandinavian fortified manors, or *gardar*. For travellers from the west, the abundance and prominence of hill-forts in the landscape was probably one of the foremost differences between their homeland and the more inland areas of the Eastern Baltic and northwestern Russia.

Most of the hill-forts in the Baltic region were located inland, having existed long before the Viking Age. Even on the Couronian coast where cultivated fields extended all the way to the sea, hill-forts could nevertheless get built in the middle of agricultural land, some twelve or more miles from the seashore. The most striking exception here is, of course, Grobiņa. The rest of the Latvian coast had very little arable land, accounting for the sparseness of population there.

The coastal hill-forts of Estonia were a different matter entirely. From the sixth to eighth centuries, a number of new hill-forts sprang up along the northern coast, along the Gulf of Finland. In fact, all the suitable harbours (with natural accessibility and good links to an affluent hinterland) in Northern Estonia, but also in Saaremaa, were marked by at least one hill-fort. Typical of pre-Viking Age and Viking Age trading posts, they were established in well-protected sea-side locations accessible by the shallow draught ships used at that time. Even better, the majority of Estonia's coastal hill-forts were located on a river bank a few miles in from the sea.

The emergence and proliferation of coastal hill-forts on Estonia's northern coast can be associated with the Eastern Way, or *Austrvegr*, which existed even before the Viking Age. These hill-forts were located alongside agricultural areas, and the adjacent settlements could have functioned as sea-sonal trading posts. The profusion of such hill-forts and set-tlements along the northern coast of Estonia, especially when contrasted to the sparsely populated southern shores of Fin-land, is a clear indication that the better route for the Eastern Way traffic ran along Estonia's northern coast. At the site of today's Tallinn the route turned north and proceeded through the Turku and the Åland archipelagos all the way to Middle Sweden. In its eastward leg the Eastern Way continued along the sparsely populated coast of present-day northwestern Russia to the Neva River and Lake Ladoga, and across Lake Ilmen, or further east to the Volga River (see Map 4 above).

In the fifth century, the trading centre of Helgö sprang up at the western end of this trading route near today's Stock-holm; the eighth century saw the rise of Birka, yet another commercial centre. In the sixth century a hill-fort was built at Iru near Tallinn (Fig. 6), and at about the same time, hill-forts emerged at Pada and Purtse in northeastern Estonia. Even more strongholds are known from the area, but sev-eral of them have yet to be excavated. All the hill-forts were accompanied by an extensive settlement, probably seasonal or semi-seasonal trading posts.

Another hill-fort that was probably part of the Eastern Way is Lyubsha on the Volkhov (or Volhov) River in northeast-ern Russia. It was erected in the second half of the seventh century and the archaeological finds resemble those from contemporary hill-forts in inland Estonia. Within a few gen-erations an initially unfortified trading post emerged about a mile upstream: Staraya Ladoga (Old Ladoga) where the earli-est finds are mostly Baltic Finnic.[11]

Figure 6. The Hill-fort of Iru in the late 1930s, photograph by
an unknown author (TLU AI fk 4047). Courtesy of the Archive of
Archaeological Research Collections, Tallinn University.

The hill-forts and settlements of the northern coast of Estonia and northwestern Russia have yielded only a handful of
items associated with long-distance trade from the period
predating the mid-ninth century. However, the amount of
Scandinavian finds and Slavic material in Staraya Ladoga
increases substantially from the middle of the ninth century
onwards, indicating a significant influx of Scandinavian colonists around then and the evolution of the settlement into an
increasingly important nodal point in both the eastern trade
and in the emerging *Garðaríki*.

Further south, several strongholds were located on the
banks of the mighty Daugava River, usually next to the rapids, of which many were virtually impassable. The period
from the sixth to eighth centuries that witnessed the rise
of *Austrvegr* was also a period of new hill-forts popping up
along the Daugava. However, as evidenced by the finds, the
intensity of long-distance traffic along the Daugava route
at that time was rather low. It was not until the start of the

tenth, and especially the eleventh century, that this water-way began to gain importance. This boost can be explained by political developments in the region that the Daugava provided access to—Kievan Rus'. We will look at this in our next chapter.

Notes

[8] Birger Nerman, *Grobin-Seeburg. Ausgrabungen und Funde* (Stockholm: Almqvist & Wiksell, 1958).

[9] *Apuolė. Ausgrabungen und Funde 1928–1932*, ed. Jan Peder Lamm (Klaipėda: Klaipėdos universiteto leidykla, 2009).

[10] King Sveigthir married a woman from *Vanalandi*. Some researchers associate *Vanalandi* with the Vanema district in northern Couronia (Jānis Asaris, Vitolds Muižinieks, Arnis Radiņš, Ingrīda Virse and Irita Žeiere, *Kurši senatnē—Couronians in Antiquity* (Riga: Latvijas Nacionālais vēstures muzejs, 2008), 139). "Vanema" means Vane-Land in the Baltic Finnic languages.

[11] Evgeny N. Nosov, "Novgorodskaya zemlja: Severnoye Priilmenye i Povolhovye," In *Rus' v. IX–X vekah. Arheologicheskaya panorama*, ed. Nikolai A. Makarov (Moskva: Drevnosti Severa, 2012), 93–119.

Chapter 3

Baltic Sea Warriors

The existence of the Eastern Way centuries before any Scandinavian expansion is proved by archaeological finds from Finland and Estonia that are associated with both Scandinavians and the eastern Finno–Ugric peoples. In western and southwestern Finland, the strong cultural impact of Scandinavia can be traced back thousands of years before the Viking Age. Second- and third-century warrior graves in Finland have yielded weapons representing international types and resembling those used in Middle Sweden during the same period. The trend strengthened further in the sixth and seventh centuries when similar modes of burial spread to parts of Estonia as well. However, jewellery deposited in graves and the general burial context retained their local character, so they are interpreted as just another element of the local Baltic Finnic culture. It is still a matter of discussion how large a proportion of warriors buried in this fashion may have been assimilated Scandinavians.

Finland in particular can boast many fifth- to seventh-century artefacts, belt mounts especially, which were manufactured by the Finno–Ugric peoples living in the Kama River basin near Perm, as far east as the foothills of the Urals. For example, a grave in the richly furnished warrior burial at Eura Pappilanmäki was equipped with belt fittings of an eastern origin as well as Scandinavian-type luxury weapons. These graves probably belonged to *Austrvegr* pioneers, warrior traders with contacts in the east and west alike.

Items originating in the Perm region have been, likewise, found in Estonia, albeit in lesser quantity—no doubt due to different funerary practices. In Finland the whole of the seventh century is considered a period marked by rich weapon burials, whereas the graves uncovered in coastal Estonia originate solely from the first half of the seventh century: here burials with grave goods almost completely ceased in the middle of the seventh century. Coastal Estonia does, however, have graves from the period between the fifth century and the first half of the seventh century, like the Proosa site near Tallinn which was furnished with Scandinavian artefacts as well as items imported from the eastern Finno-Ugric areas.

Formation of a Shared Warrior Culture in the Northern Baltic Rim

Owing to the differences in burial customs, and a lack of finds, most stray finds from coastal Estonia dated to the seventh and eighth centuries have been categorized as Finnish. The number of finds has soared recently, however, largely because of the growing use of metal detectors. It now seems that a relatively large share of the items dating from the seventh to ninth centuries is found at votive sites. Several of these finds are of the same type as those unearthed in Finland, probably indicating not just massive imports but a common Baltic Finnic cultural milieu on both coasts of the Gulf of Finland. The weapons among these finds in most cases represent the types that similarly proliferated in eastern Scandinavia.

It appears that the warriors who lived on the coasts of eastern Sweden, Finland, and Estonia must have developed close reciprocal communication, especially from the sixth and seventh centuries onwards (Fig. 7). The types of weapon that were adopted seem to indicate not just raids on each other, but also nonviolent mutual relations. Essentially, it probably meant young men entering the service of foreign chieftains, blood brotherhood, and personal friendships. Significantly, however, such alliances do not seem to have

Figure 7. Selection of five Viking Age weapons from Saaremaa, Estonia (TLU AI K 88: 143; K 85: 120; 3822: 424; K 85: 37; 4460). Photographs by M. Mägi.

extended to females. The majority of female jewellery continued to be local and unique in character.

The sixth- to eighth-century warriors of the Baltic Finnic coastal areas manifested their status through certain unique types of weapons, the same way international luxury weapons were used as status symbols. And their jewellery was altogether different. They wore large ring-headed or triangular-headed decorative pins and massive flat crossbow brooches. By the second half of the tenth century when burials in Estonia and Finland began to be accompanied with a wealth of grave goods, thus offering a better understanding of the material culture then prevalent, most of the warriors' jewellery had become almost indistinguishable from that of eastern Scandinavia. No such adoption of Scandinavian material culture occurred in the southern half of the Eastern Baltic, the territory of the ethnic Balts (Map 5).

Ornaments provide the biggest indication that the shared warrior sphere was based on more than just conflicts and adverse relations. Finds by detectorists in recent decades have included plentiful jewellery from the sixth to eighth centuries. The shapes of some of the jewellery are entirely local, specifically Baltic Finnic, whereas the ornamentation follows the Nordic animal art style (Fig. 8). Scandinavian animal art

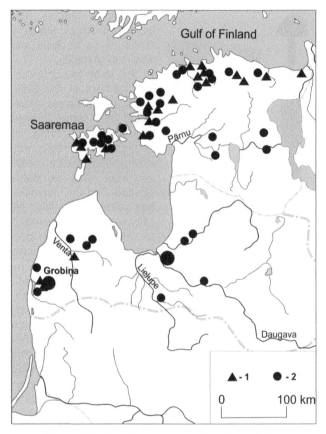

Map 5. Fifth- to tenth-century artefacts decorated in
Germanic animal styles. 1: Salin or Borre style.
2: Mammen or Ringerike style.

patterns adorned the Baltic Finnic warriors' triangular-headed
decorative pins as well as the above-mentioned flat crossbow
brooches and even certain local bracelet variations (Jets and
Mägi 2015). These apparently locally produced items and
their ornamentation prove that it was not just weaponry that

Figure 8. Local Estonian
jewellery decorated in
Germanic animal style.
1) Viidumäe, 2) Haljala,
3) Maidla (Käsmu Museum).
Photographs by I. Jets.

was adopted but also connotations and ideologies reflected
in and expressed through styles of art. At least in the Eastern
Baltic animal ornamentation functioned as an attribute man-
ifesting warrior status and distinct identity. By the tenth century at the latest the initially Scandinavian animal-art style
had spread so widely in the Baltic Finnic coastal areas that it
had become part of the local culture.

Warriors Buried in Ships

A shared warrior sphere could obviously not materialize without the movement of people. This author believes that, among
other evidence, two collective ship burials unearthed in Saaremaa a decade ago give convincing proof of this migration.

Ship burials are commonly considered predominantly
characteristic for Scandinavia, although a number of them
have turned up elsewhere, in territories culturally impacted
by the Scandinavians. Ships and boats have served as graves
for both men and women, cremated and uncremated. These
are mostly single burials but on occasion one ship has contained the remains of two or three people.

However, of the two ships found in Saaremaa, one (which, due to its small size, was actually a boat) held the remains of seven men, and the other had thirty-four bodies interred in its hull. The archaeologists who excavated the site interpreted these burials as a single event, a likely aftermath of a major battle and the simultaneous interment of a group of elite warriors from Middle Sweden.[12] The event itself was dated to the middle of the eighth century, even though the radio-carbon analysis in fact pointed to slightly different periods.

My opinion is that the bodies were placed in the burial chambers erected upon the ships not after just one event, but on multiple occasions over a longer period, perhaps even several decades. This is implied by several aspects of the burial rites, like the partly mixed bones, or around thirty cen-timetres of sand between the two layers of skeletons. While the ship burials *per se* represent Scandinavian influence, the Salme burials have a remarkable local flavour (Mägi 2018, 233–40). The ships that departed from southern Scandina-via aiming towards *Austrvegr* usually sailed from Gotland straight across the open seas and through the Salme Strait to the southern coast of Saaremaa (see Map 6). From there they would proceed to the western and northern shores of Esto-nia and present-day Russia. The Salme burials were found in a location that, by all indicators, may have been one of the several harbours dotting the southern coast of Saaremaa.

No other burials from the eighth or ninth century are known from the island, or the whole of coastal Estonia for that matter, but excavations have been conducted a few dozen miles east of Salme, in Lepna near a harbour dating from the same period. The Lepna site which was in use at least until mid-seventh century was essentially a mortuary house. Over the period of about a hundred or hundred and fifty years, the uncremated bodies of men, women, and children, proba-bly members of one family were laid to rest there. Since the structure remained standing for centuries, the bones of the deceased ended up being badly mixed and scattered.

The Salme ships, too, had stood uncovered and probably open for new interments for quite some time, until eventually

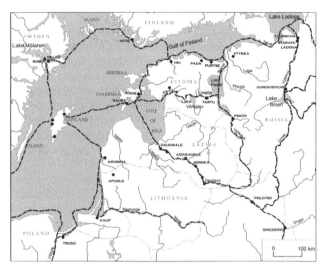

Map 6. Long-distance pre-Viking and Viking Age
trade routes through the Eastern Baltic
and places mentioned in the text.

hidden under coastal sediments—perhaps carried there by just one big storm. It is safe to assume that after a prolonged use the Salme ships would have come to resemble the local funeral houses functioning as family burial sites. The Salme finds, however, were unique in that the ships contained exclusively the remains of warriors, at least some of whom were foreign-born. In all likelihood, they were Scandinavian warriors in the service of a local chieftain, and their community was made up by their own warrior group. Local custom saw fit to bury the fallen collectively, united in death with their brothers-in-arms. And as befitting Scandinavians, they were interred in a ship, and not just in a funeral house erected on the beach.

In fact, an obvious hint at an eastern tradition of burying many warriors in one ship can be found in the mythical part of Saxo Grammaticus's *Gesta Danorum*. King Frotho was waging a war against the eastern king Olimar, also known as the king of *Ruthenia*. The Danes had occupied the islands that were "sitting between the east and Denmark", and vanquished Olimar's large fleet. After the battle, Frotho ordered that no more than ten pilots be placed in one ship because "he wished to prevent indiscriminate obsequies" (Saxo Grammaticus, 5.7.). This strange arrangement (which surely did not happen this exact way) nevertheless suggests some knowledge of the eastern tradition of burying many men in a similar fashion and in the same ship, a practice that the Scandinavians must have viewed as rather bizarre.

Once again Saxo pictures the people of *Ruthenia* as simultaneously similar to and dissimilar from Scandinavians. Hence the theory that these people were not Vikings from Scandinavia who had settled in the east, or Russians in the later meaning of the word. Indeed, they were probably Baltic Finns, men from the Eastern Way and adversaries of Swedes and Danes alike, inhabiting the coastal areas and islands of present-day Finland, Estonia, and partly also Latvia—as far as can be deduced from the ancient stories. These warriors increasingly shared the same values as their Scandinavian colleagues, formed joint warrior bands, and fought under the leadership of various chieftains on both the eastern and western shores of the Baltic Sea.

The Rus' Step onto the Stage

We may wonder who were the original *Rus'*—those who gave their name to the later Russia? Opinions differ. Western scholars mostly support the version in which the name *Rus'* is derived from the Old Norse verb *rōþs* (to row), or from the noun *rōþR* or *rōþz* (rowers, or members of an expedition of rowing ships), which appears in the toponym Roslagen (a coastal area in Middle Sweden). In its original meaning, the word has survived in the Baltic Finnic languages as their name for Sweden, for example the Finnish *Ruotsi* or Estonian *Rootsi*.

However, *Rus'* does not appear on, say, runic stones, and even sagas give it as a presumably later addition denoting the southern part of Russia (*Ruzaland*). The only exception is Saxo's *Ruthenia*, and even this can be interpreted in different ways. Some researchers, especially of Slavic extraction, have suggested that Russia's present name is derived from a southern East Slavic people, or can be associated with West Slavs or even Prussians. It is not impossible, though, to interpret it as a later fusion of variations. Take, for example, the people called *Venden* (Wends): written sources have used exactly the same name for the ones living east of Denmark, and for the ones living in Couronia and northern Latvia, although these were actually two different ethnicities.

The Russian etymologist Ageeva has pointed out that the name *Rus'* found in the Russian chronicles is linguistically in the same group with other northern, mainly Finno–Ugric ethnonyms, such as *Ves'*, *Jam'*, *Perm'*, *Lib'*, or *Chud'*. These are always used in the singular and in the feminine form, unlike the Slavic names for the southern peoples, commonly used in the plural and in the masculine form—for example *Varjagi* or *Slovene*.[13] This argument suggests that at least the *Rus'* present in the Russian chronicle texts describing the mythical period point at a northern origin.

Given that peoples along the northern Baltic shores had developed close contacts in prehistoric times long before the Viking Age, the question arises as to why the Baltic Finnic coastal dwellers should have suddenly chosen to call the Swedes "rowers". A much more credible theory is that *Rus'*, *Rhos*, or *roots* initially denoted seafarers or pirates, members of the above-described shared warrior sphere and did not denote ethnic origin. Considering the strong Scandinavian flavour defining this shared milieu it is fair to assume that the role of *lingua franca* was played by Old Norse, which would fit well with the initially North Germanic connotation of "rowers". The term would thus come into use in the Baltic Rim as a parallel name for "Viking" which originally had no ethnic context either.

The theory accentuating a social rather than an ethnic background of the original term *Rus'* has been and is supported by several researchers. The shared warrior culture thriving on the Baltic coasts which has been virtually over-looked in archaeological literature—largely for political reasons—should in this context offer supporting evidence. Depending on the individual researcher's background and theoretical persuasion, the evolution of the *Rus'* and the Eastern Way network in general has been associated with various Baltic Finnic areas showing a strong Scandinavian influence—like Åland or Northern Estonia.[14] It would make sense to assume that the early Viking Age *Rus'* came from the northern half of the Baltic Rim (Mägi 2018, 192–208). Their contingent may have included men hailing from other territories who had entered the service of *Rus'* chieftains.

The name *Rhos* first makes an appearance in written sources in the ninth century. The *Annales Bertiniani* describe events in the year 839 when a group of men who called themselves *Rhos* arrived at the Ingelheim residence of Louis the Pious, the Holy Roman Emperor, in the company of Byzantine envoys.

> He also sent with the envoys some men who said they—meaning their whole people—were called Rhos, and had been sent to him [i.e., Theophilos] by their king whose name was *chacanus*, for the sake of friendship, so they claimed. Theophilos requested in his letter that the Emperor in his goodness might grant them safe conducts to travel through his empire and any help of practical assistance they needed to return home, for the route by which they had reached Constantinople had taken them through barbarous tribes that were very fierce and savage and Theophilos did not wish them to return that way, in case some disaster befell them. When the Emperor investigated more closely the reason for their coming here, he discovered that they belonged to the people of Swedes. He suspected that they had really been sent as spies to this kingdom of ours rather than as seekers of our friendship, so he decided to keep them with him until he could find out for certain whether or not they had come in good faith. He lost no time in sending a letter to Theophilos through the same envoys to tell him all this, and to add that he had received them willingly for the sake of his friendship for Theophilos and that if they were found

to be genuine, he would supply them with means to return to their own fatherland without any risk of danger and send them home with every assistance, but if not, he would send them with envoys of ours back to Theophilos for him to deal with as he might think fit (after Duczko, *Viking Rus*, 7).

Despite this text providing the earliest known reference to the *Rhos*'s Swedish origin, several researchers have argued that the *Rhos* featured in this story did not identify themselves as Swedes (Callmer 2000, 51–52). Also, they cannot have been communicating between themselves in Old Norse—after all, it is difficult to believe that nobody recognized Old Norse in Louis's court which had relatively close contacts with the Nordic countries. The men's "Swedish origin" was established only after further examination, and was probably based on their clothing, customs, subordination, or their ability to speak some Old Norse dialect.

Some researchers have tried to interpret this episode as proof of a *Rus'* khaganate in Staraya Ladoga as early as the first half of the ninth century (Duczko 2004, 10–59). The king of the *Rus'* being called *chacanus* is indeed significant and gets repeated in several later sources. However, there is never any specific mention of any *Rus'* khaganate (Hraundal 2013, 178). It is not impossible that the habit of styling the king of the *Rus'* "khagan" was merely an explanation given by the Byzantines, based purely on the fact that this was the title used for the rulers of certain peoples (Mägi 2018, 198–206).

Peoples at the Birth of the Rus' State

Russian chronicles (of which the oldest, the so-called Primary Chronicle, was written at the start of the twelfth century) highlight a legend of three *Rus'* brothers laying the foundation for the state. In the year 859, according to this account, Varangians came from beyond the sea and took tribute from the *Chud'*, the Slovens, the Merians, and the Krivichians. The tax collectors were soon driven out, but the locals were unable to govern themselves, having descended into perpetual conflicts. That is the origin of the name for the *Rus'*.

Year 860–862 (6368–6370) [The four peoples who had been forced to pay tribute to the Varangians—*Chud'*, *Sloveni*, Merians, and Krivichians] drove the Varangians back beyond the sea, refusing them further tribute, set out to govern themselves. There was no law among them, but tribe rose against tribe. Discord thus ensued among them, and they began to war one against the other. They said to themselves, "Let us seek a prince who may rule over us, and judge us according to the Law". They accordingly went overseas to the Varangians, to the *Rus'*. These particular Varangians were known as *Rus'*, just as some other sorts are called *Sveas* [Swedes], and others Normans and Angles, and still others Gotlanders, for they were thus named. The *Chud'*, the *Sloveni*, the *Krivichians* and the *Ves'* then said to the people of *Rus'*, "Our land is great and rich, but there is no order in it. Come to rule and reign over us." They thus selected three brothers, with their kinfolk, who took with them all the *Rus'* and migrated. The oldest, Ryurik, located himself in Novgorod; the second, Sineus, in Beloozero; and the third, Truvor, in Izborsk. On account of these Varangians, the district of Novgorod became known as the land of *Rus'* (*The Russian Primary Chronicle*, chap. 1).

Two of the three brothers died, according to the chronicle, shortly after, and the third, Ryurik, became the sole ruler. Soon, in the year 882, also Kiev was subjugated.

This story is a classic foundation legend about a ruler who came from elsewhere, or was called to help, and probably has no basis in reality. However, finds of a Scandinavian character have been unearthed at several locations in Russia, and the anthroponyms and toponyms present in the Russian chronicles point at roughly the area that can be identified as the *Garðaríki* of the Norse sagas. The earliest Scandinavian impact is archaeologically visible in Staraya Ladoga, even predating the 860s mentioned in the chronicle. Elsewhere in Russia the majority of finds of Scandinavian character, like burials furnished with Scandinavian grave goods, date from the tenth century.

Remarkably, the legend clearly indicates that the invitees were not Swedes but some other "Varangians". In the later parts of the chronicles, the term *Varjagi* is occasionally used as a parallel name for the *Rus'*, while sometimes a very clear distinction is made between the two.[15]

Furthermore, a certain parallelism is found in the Russian chronicles between the ethnonyms *Rus'* and *Chud'*. However, this parallelism is restricted to the earlier period, the ninth and tenth centuries. The introductory part of the Primary Chronicle says, "In the share of Japheth lies *Rus'*, *Chud'*, and all the gentiles: *Merya, Muroma, Ves', Mordva*." (*The Primary Chronicle,* introduction). Russian researchers suggest that this list of ethnicities is likely to contain a memory of some close relations between the *Rus'* and the *Chud'* which distinguishes them both from other "peoples". According to the chronicles, the *Chud'* were among the peoples who paid tribute to the Varangians and summoned the *Rus'* to rule over them. On the other hand, they are not listed among the "peoples" who paid tribute to Prince Ryurik of the *Rus'*. Even in the tenth century events the *Chud'* are described as allies of the princes of Kievan Rus. This might point at the ethno-social original meaning of the word *Rus'*, as well as the ethno-cultural meaning of the word *Chud'*. Both terms acquired the exclusively ethnic content only in the course of time.[16]

Researchers agree that the term *Chud'* as it appears in the early Russian chronicles stands for the residents from today's Estonia along with certain Baltic Finnic neighbouring areas. The term is generally believed to be linked with early Slavic *tjudjo* (alien) and Germanic *piuða—peudo* (people).[17] As we have seen, during the Viking Age the Estonian territory fell into two distinct cultural spheres—the Scandinavian-influenced coastal Estonia, and inland Estonia with a culture similar to the present northwestern Russia. It therefore makes sense to assume that the term *Chud'* was originally exclusively associated with the inland territories and the culturally related coastal areas of northeastern Estonia. This is precisely the region that –for several other good reasons—could be subsumed under the earlier *Garðaríki*. Indeed, it seems to apply to the stories in the Russian chronicles covering the eleventh century: in these the coastal residents under attack by Russian princes are called the *Sosol'* and not the *Chud'*.[18]

According to the Russian chronicles, the alliance of the *Rus'* and the *Chud'* came to an abrupt end around 1000, which indeed coincides with a sharp decline in the archaeologically traceable Scandinavian influence within today's Russia. This period in Russia is generally perceived as one of consolidation of power and the rapid Slavonization of the elite. Contrary to what the chronicles say, it seems that the East Slavs who had congregated around Kiev in fact took over the territories of the former *Garðaríki*—and not the other way round. Sources dedicated to the eleventh century describe the *Chud'* as enemies and subject to repeated subjugation attempts by the Russian princes. This is clearly a point where the former links from Scandinavia via the eastern Baltic to the lands of the Rus' were largely severed. Let us now look at the high point of such links in the previous two centuries.

Notes

[12] Marge Konsa, Raili Allmäe, Liina Maldre, and Jüri Vassiljev, "Rescue Excavations of a Vendel Era Boat-Grave in Salme, Saaremaa," *Archeological Fieldwork in Estonia* 2008 (2009): 53–64; Jüri Peets, Raili Allmäe, and Liina Maldre, "Archaeological Investigations of Pre-Viking Age Burial Boat in Salme Village at Saaremaa," *Archeological Fieldwork in Estonia* 2010 (2011): 29–48; Jüri Peets, Raili Allmäe, Liina Maldre, Ragnar Saage, Teresa Tomek, and Lembi Lõugas, "Research Results of the Salme Ship Burials in 2011–2012,"*Archeological Fieldwork in Estonia* 2012 (2013): 43–60.

[13] R. A. Ageeva, *Strany i narody: proishozhdenie nazvaniy* (Moskva: Nauka,1990), 123–24.

14 R. A. Ageeva, *Strany i narody,* 129 and references; Elena A. Melnikova and Vladimir J. Petrukhin, "The Origin and Evolution of the Name Rus'. The Scandinavians in Eastern-European Ethno-Political Processes Before the 11th Century," *Tor* 1990–1991. 23 (1991): 203–34; Callmer, "The Archaeology of the Early Rus'."

[15] Elena A. Melnikova, *Drevnyaya Rus' i Skandinaviya. Izbrannoye trudy. Old Rus' and Scandinavia. Selected Papers* (Moskow: Dmitriy Pozharskiy University, 2011), 71.

[16] Melnikova and Petrukhin, "The Origin and Evolution of the Name Rus'."

[17] R. A. Ageeva, *Strany i narody*, 86–115.

[18] Probably from the Old Norse name for these areas—*Syslar* (Mägi 2018, 381–84).

Chapter 4

The High-Point of Scandinavian Eastward Activity

The various Baltic peoples' mercantile connections with the east received a major boost in the second half of the ninth century, and most of the tenth century was characterized by a boom in eastern trade. It was during this period that large amounts of silver poured into the Baltic Rim from Arabic countries. Part of the silver was probably melted down and recast, some has survived to this day in the shape of so-called Kufic coins or dirhams.

Most researchers agree that the main commodities the Baltic countries exported to the Arabic world in return for silver were furs and slaves. Mention has already been made of swords sold to Arabic countries by the *ar-Rus* merchants; however, these cannot have played any major role in the suddenly blossoming eastern trade.

The economies of most Muslim countries needed an extensive slave workforce to function properly, and sources often mention blond and blue-eyed slaves. At that time, fair-haired people inhabited the territories of modern Finland and the Baltics, Scandinavia, Belarus, and Ukraine rather than the northern part of modern-day Russia. The Eastern Way to the Volga River normally did not go through Belarus or Ukraine, so it is reasonable to assume that the fair-haired slaves sold at the Bulgar markets were kidnapped from the shores of the Baltic during raids.

Trade Routes and Hoards

Judging by archaeological material, especially hoards and their composition, it seems that in the tenth century the predominant long-distance trade route through modern Russian territory was the Eastern Way reaching from the Baltic Sea through the Gulf of Finland to the Volga River, and then southwards to the Middle East. No doubt the other route, leading along the Dnieper River to the Black Sea and Constantinople—the so-called "route from the Varangians to the Greeks" to quote the Primary Chronicle—also saw lively traffic. The dearth of Byzantine coins and absence of Byzantine imports in the Baltic Rim have inspired suggestions of a much lower intensity of traffic on this particular route in the tenth century as compared to the eleventh. This theory seems to be supported by similar patterns in the archaeological finds from the surroundings of the Daugava River, which served as the main access from the Baltic Sea to the Dnieper and also saw a major upsurge in usage from the eleventh century onwards.

Therefore, it is by no means surprising that in the ninth and tenth centuries, hill-forts flourished along the Eastern Way, that is, on the Estonian islands and northern coast. The key role that hill-forts played in international trade seems to be confirmed by the dirham hoards found in their vicinity (Map 7). Indeed, the ninth- and tenth-century dirham hoards unearthed in the Eastern Baltic are noticeably concentrated on Åland and around the hill-forts of Northern Estonia and Saaremaa. These hoards, as a rule, turn up in the fields near the strongholds—most probably marking the homesteads of the local landowners–traders.

Furthermore, in Estonia dirham hoards have been unearthed in the vicinity of the major Viking Age trading centre of Tartu in the eastern part of the country, and in fields along the Pärnu River. This east–west route followed the rivers of central Estonia and was presumably used mostly during the winter freeze. Hoards consisting exclusively of dirhams have been found in the lower reaches of the Daugava and around Grobiņa in Couronia, yet are very rare elsewhere in the Eastern Baltic. So, the ninth- and tenth-century hoards clearly trace the important Viking Age trade routes, as far as we can topographically identify those routes.

The Eastern Way Marked with Hill-Forts

The trading centre of Birka in Middle Sweden that stood until about 975 and was then burned down had links to the Eastern Way. From Birka and Lake Mälaren, both directly inland from Stockholm, ships would proceed to the Åland archipelago which has yielded numerous dirham hoards and rich tenth-century archaeological material. Judging by the latter, during the Viking Age Åland's population was composed of Scandinavians, with some Finnish and Estonian influence (*The Viking Age in Åland*, ed. Ahola).

In Finland the only archaeologically excavated landing site that had connections with the Eastern Way is located at Hitis (Finnish "Hiittinen") in the Turku archipelago. However, sites of Scandinavian character have been found in abundance all over southwestern Finland. Among similar sites in northern Estonia, perhaps the most thoroughly investigated is the Iru complex near Tallinn which consists of a hill-fort and an adjacent settlement. Tallinn Bay provides a good natural environment for a harbour, linked by a river to the fertile arable lands of Harjumaa a few miles inland.

Sitting upon the naturally well-protected steep river bend a few miles from the ancient shoreline, the Iru hill-fort seems to have had its heyday in the ninth century: the most extensive and intense cultural layer present in the stronghold dates from this particular period. The hill-fort burned down multiple times over the centuries, and one of the more devastating fires seems to have taken place around 900. After a while the hill-fort was rebuilt, though a quarter the size of before, and with stronger fortifications. Iru was abandoned for good at the start of the eleventh century.[19]

Recent research has proved the existence of a possible harbour near Tallinn during the Viking Age, and even earlier. It was a likely stopover for ships sailing along the Eastern

Way without any intention of visiting the local trading post upstream. The same pattern can be detected with several other northern Estonian settlement complexes: one hill-fort stood close to the sea on the river bank and another, usually a bigger one, further upstream—probably serving as a trading post in close proximity to the winter roads crossing the nearby wetlands in winter. This was the case with the two hill-forts at Pada in northeastern Estonia. Archaeological excavations indicate that the Viking Age hill-fort of Pada was abandoned around 1000.

In northeastern Estonia, the most suitable harbour site was Purtse—marked, too, by two hill-forts, one of them around two hundred and fifty metres from the sea. While the smaller one has not been archaeologically investigated, excavations at the bigger of the two, the remarkably well-defended Purtse Tarakallas, indicate its survival long after the Viking Age. This stronghold was accompanied by a large settlement. Also, a hill-fort and trade centre complex probably existed in the district around the modern town of Narva. The area has yielded plenty of Viking Age finds but the site itself has been completely destroyed by later construction works.

The sparsely populated coastal region that is now northwestern Russia started immediately beyond Narva. It was here, ten kilometres from the shore that the Viking Age hill-fort of Vtyrka stood on the edge of fields. Like many other strongholds in the neighbourhood it was abandoned at the start of the eleventh century.[20] A little farther away, the sites on the banks of the Volkhov River saw major changes around 900. At about that time, the Staraya Ladoga trading centre, home to a considerable number of Scandinavians as evidenced by archaeological finds, was fortified with an earthen wall. It is hardly a coincidence that soon afterwards, the outpost of this new fortified settlement, the Lyubsha hill-fort a few kilometres downstream, lost its purpose and was abandoned. The growing power of Scandinavians on the Volkhov River that took travellers inland from Lake Ladoga was also expressed through Ryurik's settlement of Gorodishche near the later Novgorod. Strongly Scandinavian in character,

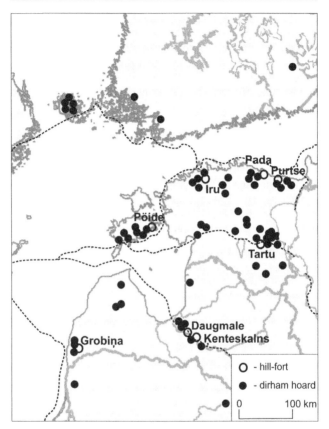

Map 7. Ninth- to tenth-century hoards consisting of dirhams,
the most intensively used long-distance trade routes,
and key hill-forts along these routes.

Gorodishche took root in the middle of the ninth century but
was equally quickly deserted for a period at the start of the
eleventh century.[21]

The course of the Eastern Way that crossed the island of Gotland and proceeded to the southern part of Scandinavia was during the Viking Age delineated by the strongholds of Padise in northwestern Estonia and Pöide in Saaremaa. Both were abandoned around 1000 but were refortified later in the Middle Ages. The rest of Estonia's hill-forts had no direct links with sea routes.

Slave Markets in Austrvegr

The most detailed description of tenth-century Estonia is found in the Saga of Óláf Tryggvason (*The Saga of Óláf Tryggvason*, chaps. 5–7). The saga speaks of King Óláf of Norway who spent six years of his childhood in the 960s or 970s as a slave in Estonia. A shorter version is given in *A History of Norway*:

> [the Norwegian travelling party with three-year-old Óláf] made for Russia but landed in Estonia. In the end while sailing off *Eisisla* [Saaremaa] they were intercepted by pirates and some of them taken prisoner, some killed. Among them the boy's foster-father was also executed, while the boy Óláf himself was sold as a slave to Estonians. Óláf was redeemed from there by a kinsman of his who by chance was sent there at that time by the king of Russia with the task of collecting taxes (*A History of Norway*, 19).

A much longer passage in the same saga, probably written down decades later, provides further details, including the names of the princely slave's masters and the price paid for the boy. It also describes in greater detail how the boy was freed from slavery.

> Sigurth Eiríksson came to Estland, being sent there by King Valdamar of *Hólmgarðr* to fetch from that land the tribute due to the king. Sigurth travelled in great state, accompanied by many men and with much money. In the market place he saw a boy of great beauty, and surmised that he probably was a foreigner there, and asked him about his name and kin. He gave his name a Óláf, and said his father was Tryggvi Óláfsson, and his mother, Ástríth, daughter of

Eirík Bjóthaskalli. Than Sigurth understood that the boy was his sister's son. He asked the boy how he had got there, and Óláf told him all that happened to him. Sigurth asked him to come with him to farmer Réás' [Óláf's owner] place. And when he arrived there he bought both boys, Óláf and Thorgísl, and took them with him to *Hólmgarðr* (*The Saga of Óláf Tryggvason*, chap. 6).

The text makes fascinating reading in other respects. For example, *Estland* is pictured as an integral part of the Viking world, and a link between Scandinavia and *Garðaríki*: King Valdemar of *Garðaríki*, himself a historical figure, sends his tax collectors there. Notably, judging by the saga, Scandinavians did not have linguistic problems in communicating with Estonians. In view of the common cultural sphere of warriors shown in the archaeological material, mutual language skills were a very strong possibility.

As the story goes, Estonians acted like Vikings, attacking the passing ships and trading in the markets of Novgorod—in the 960s the location would actually have been Staraya Ladoga or Ryurik's Gorodishche. For it was there that the twelve-year-old Óláf purportedly met the Estonian Viking who had killed his stepfather. The boy took his revenge by slaying the man.

The Saga of Óláf Tryggvason further describes Estonian harbours and local markets selling slaves, among other goods. Óláf's mother Ástríth spent nine years enslaved in Estonia, and was only freed after a visiting Norwegian merchant Lothin recognized his former queen up for sale in a slave market.

Often he [Lothin] went on trading journeys, and sometimes, on Viking expeditions. One summer Lothin went on trading journey in the Baltic with only one ship, laden with much merchandise. He sailed to *Estland* and there attended markets during the summer. And when there was a market, all kinds of wares were brought there, and many bondwomen were there for sale. Lothin saw a woman there who had been sold as a slave. And when he looked at the woman he recognized her and knew her to be Ástríth, the daughter of Eirík, who had been King Tryggvi's wife, though she looked

Figure 9. Excavations at Daugmale hill-fort in 1937.
Photograph by V. Ģinters (LVNM excavation reports AA 460).
Courtesy of the National History Museum of Latvia.

different from what she had done when last he saw her. She was pale and peaked and poorly clad. He went up to her and asked how matters stood with her. She replied, "It is bitter to tell you about it. I am sold as a slave, and brought here to be sold." [...] Lothin bought Ástríth and took her home to Norway with him (*The Saga of Óláf Tryggvason*, chap. 52).

Seeing as Lothin arrived on a ship, the marketplace is likely to have been located near a settlement in northern Estonia or Saaremaa, like Purtse or Tallinn. The whole of Estonia's coast probably had no more than a handful of naturally endowed landing places with a proper hinterland able to support an international marketplace.

Estonian coastal hill-forts have been mentioned by name in the Norse sagas only once, in a tale of Icelandic Vikings fighting some other seafarers, or perhaps warships defending the local shores near *Rafala* (*The Story of Burnt Njal*, chap. 30). Of course, it is possible that the saga's *Rafala* refers not so much to present-day Tallinn (known as Revel in Hanseatic times) as to the surrounding area at large. Saxo Grammaticus, on the other hand, puts names to the hill-forts dotting the coast—and judging by his Latin toponyms they were all located in *Ruthenia*. Whatever the case may be, Saxo's recountings of old tales spoke of the hill-forts of *Austrvegr* and *Estland* or *Eysýsla*—both of which are frequently brought up in sagas as well. It is obviously impossible to find out what these hill-forts were actually called in the ninth and tenth centuries.

Hill-Forts along the Daugava Way

The Daugava River is the largest waterway passing through the Eastern Baltic. It leads first to Polotsk and from there across the watershed to the Dnieper River, and so on to Kiev, the seat of Russian princes. Still further downstream were the Black Sea and Constantinople.

Sprinkled with hundreds of rapids, the Daugava was actually rather difficult to navigate. As a rule, the larger rapids where the boats had to be hauled ashore or pulled with ropes had a hill-fort standing guard. While negotiating the rapids the travellers were easy prey for attackers, and those who came in peace most probably preferred paying tolls to the local chieftains.

Damming the river to produce hydroelectric power has nowadays caused most of the Daugava rapids to disappear. Also, many sites have been flooded as a result of building—though, some hasty rescue excavations were undertaken at a few of them.

The watershed of the Daugava was marked by fields that started about ten miles from the seashore, while the river's southern bank was a forested area unsuitable for agriculture and stretching eastward, upstream, for about a hundred kilometres or so. Arable lands were concentrated on the northern bank which was a predominantly Livic area by the end of the prehistoric period. Some Latvian archaeologists theorize that the lower reaches of the Daugava were inhabited by Semgallians right through till the late Viking Age (Radiņš 1998). However, the fertile fields and Semgallian sites from the historical Semgallia were separated from the Daugava by a barren, largely uninhabited zone some thirty kilometres wide.

The banks of the Daugava are dotted with hill-forts, several of them perching on high promontories on the river's northern side, some complete with large settlements in the vicinity. While hoards dating from the ninth and tenth centuries have been unearthed around the lower Daugava, burials seem to be almost non-existent until the mid-tenth century. In this sense the region resembles the *Austrvegr* territories inhabited by Baltic Finns which similarly feature only a few burials predating the end of the Viking Age.

Perhaps the best known among the hill-forts in the Livic territory along the lower Daugava is Daugmale, sitting on the southern bank amongst fields and in close proximity of the river rapids (Fig. 9). Like many other Daugava hill-forts, Daugmale was used over an extensive period of time, and has an intense cultural layer dating from the Viking Age and especially from the eleventh and twelfth centuries. The hill-fort was accompanied by a settlement and a harbour site, and the whole complex may have formed a network with the settlements and cemeteries located across the river.

Some researchers have suggested that in the ninth and tenth centuries Daugmale was home to the Semgallian people (Radiņš 1998).[22] However, the Viking Age artefacts that are commonly considered Semgallian and are considered as confirmation of the hypothesis have a much wider spread and are also characteristic of finds on the Estonian island of Saaremaa, for example. Notwithstanding, it may certainly be possible to speak of multi-ethnic inhabitation at Daugmale after the second half of the tenth century, when ethnic diversity becomes visible in the burials.

Another important Viking Age Livic centre on the Daugava is the large hill-fort and settlement complex of Aizkraukle—and in fact there are many more. The lands east of Aizkraukle on either side of the river were inhabited by Latgallians and the Seli people and marked by a multitude of hill-forts and settlements as well as spacious cemeteries with plentiful inhumation burials dating especially from the seventh century onwards. The archaeological material from these sites shows a sudden surge at the start of the eleventh century. A number of ninth- and tenth-century hill-forts were abandoned around 1000, like Dignāja on the southern bank of the Daugava; its role was taken over by the Latgallian centre Jersika on the opposite bank (Šnē 2006).

Most researchers agree that in the ninth and tenth centuries the Daugava waterway played a less important role in international communication than it did in the centuries that followed (Radiņš 1998). Around Polotsk and the watershed between the Western Dvina (the Belarusian name for the Daugava) and Dnieper rivers in today's Belarus and Russia, the early tenth century witnessed the appearance in abundance of items of Scandinavian character, increasingly so as the century progressed.[23] Many researchers, conversely, argue that the most popular tenth-century connection between Polotsk and the Baltic Sea was the route along the large lakes of Estonia and Russia and the Velikaya River which runs through Pskov. In this area, similarly, the presence of Scandinavians can be observed from the end of the ninth century until the early eleventh century.[24]

In the Norse sagas the Daugava, described as part of *Austrvegr*, features under the name *Dýnu*[25] and also appears in the stories of Saxo Grammaticus. In his books about the mythological kings, the Daugava is called *Hellespont*, and the most prominent hill-fort on the river, probably located on its lower reaches, is dubbed *Duna* (Saxo Grammaticus, 1.6.10.) Saxo and the anonymous authors of the sagas now and again mention communication between the Daugava region and Kievan Rus—to where the river leads, after all. This supports the contention that the tenth century saw a heightened activity of Scandinavians on the Daugava waterway, although it was probably comparatively less than on the routes passing the Estonian and Finnish coasts.

Vikings Plundering Couronia

In Couronia, Scandinavian-style finds seem to dry up during the period after the desertion of the Grobiņa Scandinavian colony, especially when compared to the northern half of the Eastern Baltic. The handful of dirham hoards found in this region hail from the vicinity of Grobiņa and serve as proof of continued use of the hill-fort complex by the local Cours.

Couronia is generally overlooked in saga literature. Indeed, for those whose destination was the Volga or the Dnieper, Couronia's long and straight coastline was nowhere near the main routes. On the other hand, it is again Saxo Grammaticus who knows a lot about Couronia and its inhabitants—though it is not clear whether he is referring to the Couronian region in modern Latvia and Lithuania, or to a broader area that also incorporated the Kura Island, or Saaremaa in today's Estonia. Phrases like "Vikings plundering Denmark, such as *Kúrir* and others from *Austrvegr*" (*Knytlinga Saga*, chap. 29) that we encounter, especially, in the chronicles dealing with Denmark may imply that the term *Kuri* was occasionally used to designate, in a broader sense, pirates from the east. If for topographic reasons alone, "others from *Austrvegr*" can be identified as inhabitants of Estonia's coastal areas; in these sagas Finland appears to remain mainly outside *Austrvegr*.

Couronia does seem to make an appearance in Egil's Saga, making up for the general oversight in Icelandic sagas. Egil's Saga gives a long and detailed, in places almost ethnographic, description of a Viking raid to Couronia in 936.

> Thorof and Egil were held in high favour by Thorir over the winter and in the spring they fitted out a great longship and gathered a crew and in the summer sailed into *Austrvegr* and raided and plundered and fought in many encounters. They continued as far as *Kurland* and lay to there for a fortnight's rest and trade. And when this ended, they began to raid again and went ashore at various places.
>
> One day they lay to in the mouth of a great river with a dense forest on the shores. They made plans to go ashore there and split into parties of twelve men each. They went

into the forest and it was not long before they came to a first settlement. There they pillaged and killed some men but most of the inhabitants ran off and they met no real resistance. [...]

Egil had gone through the forest with twelve men and then they saw great expanses of open land with settlements. There was a farm a little way off from them and they headed for it and when they came up to it they ran into the buildings but found no one there and they seized what valuables were lying about. There were many buildings and this took them a long time and, when they had come out and moved off from the farm buildings, a group of people had gathered between them and the woods and were advancing on them. A high palisade rose between them and the woods. Then Egil told them to follow him so that they could not be attacked from all sides.

Egil and his men then got caught by the locals, were shut in some sort of storage house, and left to await their fate.

The man who owned that farm was rich and powerful and he had a grown son. Then there was talk as to what was to be done with the prisoners. The farmer said that he thought it advisable that they should be killed one after the other. The farmer's son said that night was falling and that there would be no entertainment in torturing them. He asked that they should let things be until morning. They were then pushed into a building and tightly bound.

However, the Vikings were able to escape aided by a slave called Aki and his sons.

They then came into another room. This too had log walls. They heard men's voices from below under their feet. They searched about and found a trap door in the floor. They raised it up and below was a deep pit from which they heard the voices. Then Egil asked who was there. A man who called himself Aki answered.

Egil asked whether he wanted to get out of the pit. Aki replied that that they gladly would. Then Egil and his companions let the ropes that they had been tied with down into the pit and pulled up three men. Aki said that the other two were his sons and that they were Danes who had been captured the previous summer. "I was well treated over the winter", he said, "and was kept busy tending the farmers' stock but the boys were made to work as slaves and didn't like that. In the spring we made plans to run off but we were caught. Then we were put here in this pit." (after Sayers, "A Glimpse of Medieval Curonian Vernacular Architecture").

With help from Aki, the Norwegian Vikings managed to loot the place. Having fled to the safety of the nearby forest, Egil soon returned and torched the manor house along with the men feasting inside.

This story is unusual for the plethora of detail in its descriptions of the buildings (including their architecture and functions) and the dwellers on a large Couronian farm. Communicated through a transcription made two hundred years later and thus probably inaccurate, it nevertheless offers a rare portrait of a wealthy household in the Viking Age Eastern Baltic. Judging by topography, the episode probably took place somewhere on the lower reaches of the Venta River, a sandy and forested area with good arable lands and, in all likelihood, a wealthy farming community.

Two Periods of Transformation

Two major periods of change can be detected in the Viking Age archaeological material recovered from the Eastern Baltic. One such period fell at the end of the ninth century or around 900 when some of the hill-forts lining the trade routes were burned down, and others fortified. This period also saw the dawn of most of the Scandinavian colonies in the territory of what later became known as Russia (Pushkina 2004). Discernible since the seventh century, the Scandinavians' eastern interests expanded further at the end of the ninth century, and it was hardly a peaceful process.

The other notable turning point came around 1000 when most of the Eastern Way hill-forts in the coastal areas of Estonia and northwestern Russia were abandoned. Coincidentally, a number of other North European trading centres were either burned down or deserted. At the start of the eleventh century, the archaeologically visible presence of Scandinavians in Russia declined abruptly and their colonies ceased to exist, even though written sources suggest the continuation of close contacts throughout the eleventh century. Whatever the reality, the new millennium probably witnessed the rise of the originally Scandinavian Varangians who assimilated fast but were not numerous enough to leave any archaeological traces worthy of mention.

The influx of dirhams into eastern Scandinavia for the most part stopped around 960, though some coins that have come to light so far can be dated to a later period. The last Kufic coins that reached the Eastern Baltic were minted at the start of the eleventh century, and in Russia the last dirhams date from the mid-eleventh century. Arabian silver was mostly replaced by coins minted in Western Europe. In certain regions on the Eastern Way—like Åland—hoards and archaeological finds on the whole disappeared in the early eleventh century.

Several theories have been proposed to explain the cessation of the dirham trade. However, in the light of what we have seen above it was probably Scandinavians themselves that lost interest in the Volga waterway and Arabic silver imports. The state-making process and conversion to Christianity facilitated the incorporation of Scandinavian kingdoms into the Western European cultural space—and thus provided easier access to western silver. Equally, the Russian princes were unlikely to tolerate the uncontrollable activity of Viking bands in their principalities, so, having secured their authority, they promptly took firm control of long-distance trade.

Both of these periods of change thus seem to be associated with the role of Scandinavians in eastern trade and eastern policies. These processes have left a clear impact on the Estonian and Latvian archaeological material. The abandonment of many Estonian hill-forts and trading places at the start of the eleventh century led to a transformation of the cultural landscape. The second half of the eleventh century witnessed the rise of new and much larger hill-forts, some erected near the former strongholds on the coast, and others built to guard over the winter roads now in intensive use.

It is certainly no coincidence that around 1000, the *Chud'*, then probably inhabitants of inland Estonia and, according to the Russian chronicles, allies of the *Rus'*, were suddenly redefined as "enemies" of Russian princes. The abrupt decline of Scandinavian influence in the east and the shifting of popular trade routes went hand in hand with the political consolidation and Slavonization of Kievan Rus—a process that indeed appears to have created conflicts. At any rate, at the start of the eleventh century Russian princes made multiple attempts to subjugate inland Estonia, or at least re-establish some influence over the region, but without success. Norse sagas imply that Scandinavian kingdoms too, Sweden in particular, were fighting for supremacy in the coastal areas of *Austrvegr*.

The turn of the first millennium saw the end of the highpoint of Viking trade. From then on, the trade was mainly carried on between the Scandinavian kingdoms and the Russian princedoms. This proved to be the end of an era.

Notes

[19] Valter Lang, *Muistne Rävala. Muistised, kronoloogia ja maaviljelusliku asustuse kujunemine Loode-Eestis, eriti Pirita jõe alamjooksu piirkonnas* [Prehistoric Rävala: Antiquities, Chronology and the Establishment of Farming Settlement in North-West Estonia, with special reference to the area on the lower reaches of the Pirita River], 2 vols. (Tallinn: Eesti Teaduste Akadeemia, 1996), 101–4.

[20] Elena R. Mikhaylova, "Gorodische na Vtyrke," in *Élite ou Égalité. Northern Rus' and Cultural Transformations in Europe in the 600–1300 A.D.*, ed. N. I. Platonova (Sankt-Peterburg: Branko, 2017), 261–82, available at http://www.archeo.ru/izdaniya-1/vagnejshije-izdanija/pdf/2017Elite.pdf, accessed January 21, 2019.

[21] Evgeny N. Nosov, B. M. Goryunova, and A. V. Plohov, *Gorodishche pod Novgorodom i poseleniya severnova Priilmenya* (Sankt-Peterburg: Russkaya Akademya Nauk, 2005), 28.

[22] See also Arnis Radiņś, "Lower Daugava Area," in *Transforma-*

tio Mundi, ed. Bertašius, 81–92; Guntis Zemītis, "10th–12th Century Daugmale. The Earliest Urban Settlement along the Lower Daugava and Forerunner of Riga," in *Cultural Interaction Between East and West*, ed. Fransson, 279–84.

[23] Ivan I. Eremeev, "North European Objects of the 9th–11th Centuries from the Upper Reaches of the Western Dvina and the 'Route from the Varangians to the Greeks'," in *Cultural Interaction Between East and West*, ed. Fransson, 250–62.

[24] Sergei Beletzki, *Nachalo Pskova* (Sankt-Peterburg: RAN Institut Istory Materialnoy Kultury, 1996).

[25] Daugava in German is Düna, and in Baltic Finnic languages Väina ("Sound"), which seems to be connected with the name *Hellespontos* that Saxo had chosen for it, since classical Hellespont was the narrow strait at the Dardanelles.

Chapter 5

End of the Viking Age

Several Scandinavian researchers date the end of the Viking Age to the period around 1000 when these societies had formed a state and converted to Christianity. Other researchers propose the mid-eleventh century or even later, around 1100. The eleventh century was indeed a time of crucial changes. Whereas the first quarter of the century was still dominated by old Viking Age patterns, the second half saw a completely different social and political situation emerge.

Beginning of a New Era

Although long-distance trade to the Volga River had waned by the eleventh century, the commercial relations between Scandinavia and Russia continued to strengthen and expand. The Dnieper waterway leading to Kiev and Byzantium was more popular than ever, and the role played by Russian principalities as individual markets kept growing steadily.

From the late tenth century onwards, the burials of Baltic Finns were accompanied by an abundance of grave goods, which has dramatically improved the general knowledge of late Viking Age material culture in the northern half of the Eastern Baltic. Admittedly, the warrior culture characterizing the Baltic Finnic coastal areas was by that time strongly reminiscent of eastern Scandinavia. However, the female attributes and the culture of inland areas as a whole retained their local and ethnic characteristics. By the eleventh and twelfth

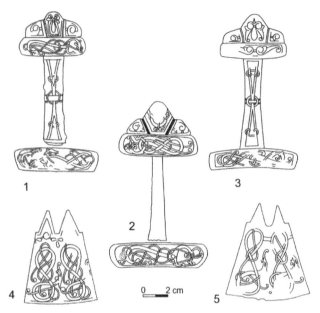

Figure 10. Selection of ornaments from Estonian sword hilts and spearhead sockets. 1: Maidla (AM 839: 1, 2), 2: Karja parish (in private possession), 3: Kurevere (TLU AI 4368: 38), 4: Lehts (TLU AI 3937), 5: Saaremaa (TLU AI K 85: 116). From: Jets, Indrek. 2013. Lahingu maod. Skandinaavia 9–11. sajandi sajandi kunstistiilid Eesti arheoloogilistel leidudel. Tallinna Ülikooli Kirjastus: Tallinn, Figs. 46, 48: 2, 61: 1–4. Drawn by I. Jets.

centuries, Scandinavian-type ornaments, warriors' jewellery, and weapons had all become an inherent part of the local culture, designed and produced locally (Fig. 10).

No doubt personal relations thrived between the warriors and chieftains on the opposite sides of the Baltic Rim, increasingly overshadowed, though, by the fact that Scandinavians were now Christians while most of the Eastern Baltic was still heathen. Given that the Russian principalities east of the Baltic were also Christian, the Baltic region formed a sort of heathen buffer zone between the Western and Eastern churches, between Scandinavia and the Russian states, both trying to take possession of the lands that comprise modern-day Estonia. Similar attempts were probably made on the Daugava Way, although no written sources are available to confirm this.

In 1007 the young Prince Óláf Haraldsson, the future King Óláf of Norway, also known as Saint Óláf, embarked on an ambitious Viking expedition, first attacking Sweden and then progressing to Sweden's dominions. Pushed back from Lake Mälaren, the Norwegians spent the winter in Gotland, from where they proceeded to Saaremaa in 1008, and thereafter raided the Finnish shores.

Here we are told that as soon as spring arrived, King Óláf sailed east to *Eysýsla* to harry. He went up on land, but the men of *Eysýsla* came down to the shore and fought with them. King Óláf was victorious there, he pursued them, harried, and devastated the land. We are told that at first, when King Óláf arrived in *Eysýsla*, the farmers offered to pay tribute. But when they arrived with the tribute he marched against them with his troops fully armed; and then it turned out otherwise than the farmers had expected; for they had come down to the shore, not with the tribute, but rather, all armed, and gave battle to the king, as was told before.

Afterwards he sailed back to Finland, harried there, and invaded the country, and all the people fled into the forests, emptying their homes of all property. The king went far inland and through some forests, until they came to some valley settlements, called *Herdalar*. There they found little property and no people. The day wore on, and the king returned toward his ships. But when they passed through the forest, they were attacked fiercely from all sides with arrow shots. The king bade his men protect themselves as best they could and advance against the enemy, but that was difficult as the Finns hid behind trees. And before the king left the forest behind, he had lost many men, and many were wounded before he reached the ships late in the evening. During the night, the Finns with their witchcraft made a furious gale and a storm at sea. But the king bade his men weigh anchor and hoist the sails and cruise before the land during the night. And then, as often afterwards, the king's luck prevailed over the magic of the Finns. During the night they cruised along *Bálagardsside* and from there out to sea. The army of the Finns followed them on land as the king sailed outside (*Saint Óláf's Saga*, chaps. 7–9).

In 1075, Adam of Bremen referred to Estonia (*Aestland*) as one of the Swedish "islands", and in 1123, certain sources identified Estonia (*Hestia*) and Finland (*Findia*) as Sweden's "eastern provinces" (Adam of Bremen, chap. 4:17).[26]

A History of Norway, on the other hand, claims the young Prince Óláf resided in Novgorod instead:

> Because he was dispossessed of his native land, he [Prince Óláf] had to turn to piracy. He usually wintered in a town, which we call *Hólmgarðr*, attended by his numerous fleet. In summer he constantly harassed all the peoples round *Mare Balticum* [the Baltic Sea] with raiding and ravaging. He utterly laid waste the large and populous island of *Eysýsla*, and so harried two others equal to it in size and population, namely *Gotland* and *Eyland*, that their inhabitants paid enormous sums in tribute throughout the time he stayed in Russia. In the country of *Curi* [Couronians] he inflicted no small slaughter on them, crowned with most glorious success (*A History of Norway*, chap. 23:20–31).[27]

This narrative, likewise, indicates that the prince plundered the coastal areas that could, judging by archaeological as well as written evidence, be considered a Swedish dominion. No mention, however, is made of the coastal areas that presumably fell under the realm of *Garðaríki*. His "numerous fleet" probably wintered somewhere on a Baltic Sea coast rather than Novgorod (*Hólmgarðr*), which seems impossible, geographically.

Struggle for the Former Dominions in the Eastern Baltic

According to *Heimskringla*, ten years after Prince Óláf's raid, in 1017, a *ting* assembly was called in Uppsala where the

King of Sweden Olaf Skötkonung was accused of letting go of the eastern scat-lands, that is land for which tribute was payable.

> Thorgný [the spokesman for the Swedish peasants] spoke as follows: "Different is now the disposition of the Swedish kings from what it was before. Thorgný, my father's father, remembered Eirík Emundarson, king in Uppsala, and related this about him that when he was in his best years he had a levy every summer and proceeded to various lands, subjecting to his sway *Finnland* and *Kirjálaland*, *Estland* and *Kúrland* and wide reaches of other lands in the east. And one may still see the fortifications and other great works which he made (there). [...] Thorgný, my father, was a long time with King Bjorn, and he knew his way of dealing with men. And while Bjorn lived his dominion flourished and in nowise decreased. [...] I myself can remember King Eirík the Victorious, for I was with him in many warlike expeditions. He increased the dominion of the Swedes and defended it valiantly. [...]
>
> But the king whom we now have lets no one presume to talk to him except about what he himself wants done; and on that alone he is intent, but lets lands tributary to him defect from him through his lack of energy and enterprise. [...] Now if you intend to regain those lands in the east which your kinsmen and forbears have possessed there, then we shall all follow your leadership to do so. But if you will not do as we say, we shall set upon you and kill you, and not tolerate from you lawlessness and hostility." (*Saint Óláf's Saga*, chap. 80).

The saga never mentions the episode again, but it is apparently based on other, surviving narratives confirming that the king of Sweden indeed tried to take steps to regain the lost eastern dominions: he sent his son Onund, accompanied by his friend Yngvar, to claim the unpaid tributes.

> There was a dispute between King Olaf and that people who are called *Seimgalir*, and they had not paid tax for some time. Then King Olaf sent Onund and Yngvar with three ships to demand tribute.

They reach land and call a meeting with the inhabitants, and there they demanded tribute from their king. [...] The king (of *Seimgalir*) and many other chiefs saw no choice but to pay the tax which was demanded, all except three chiefs who did not want to follow the king's advice and refused to pay the tax and raised an army.

But when the king heard what they were up to, he asked Onund and Yngvar to fight them and gave them troops. They fought, and there was great loss of life there before they put the chiefs to flight. In the rout, the chief who had most opposed the paying of tribute was taken captive, and they hanged him, but the other two got away. They took much booty there and claimed all the tributes, and, that done, they sailed back to King Olaf and brought him a great wealth of gold and silver and good treasures (*Saga of Ingvar the Traveller*, chap. 4).

Like several other sagas, this story represents a certain discrepancy between the written sources and archaeological evidence. *Seimgalir* is usually believed to be Semgallia which is an ethnic Baltic inland region with its own unique culture and fertile lands, connected to the sea by the Lielupe River. Topographically, Semgallia is nowhere near important international trade routes, and it has yielded fewer Scandinavian finds than several other areas in the Eastern Baltic.

In all the Norse sagas, this is the only story to mention the presumed Semgallia, and it is not impossible that the toponym *Semgalir* has been added by a later narrator. At any rate, it is quite plausible that Sweden indeed took certain action to reclaim its eastern dominions.

Attempts to subjugate the Baltics are even more explicitly manifested in the Russian chronicles. In 1030, Yaroslav the Wise, Prince of Kiev, conquered the principal trading centre in inland Estonia, Tartu, and transformed it into his administrative hub (*The Russian Primary Chronicle*, year 1030 (6538)). In the 1050s, Russian princes invaded the coastal area of Harjumaa. This region is called *Syslar* in Scandinavian chronicles and its inhabitants referred to as *Sosol'* by the Russian sources. In the year 1060 the *Sosol'* were forced to pay tributes to the Russians; however, in the spring of 1061 they attacked Tartu, burned it down and plundered the surrounding areas all the way to Pskov.

> Izyaslav Yaroslavich waged war on the *Sosol'* and he ordered them to pay a tax of 2000 *grivnas*. They promised to do so, but later they expelled the tax collectors. Then in spring they waged war around *Yuryev*, setting fire to the fort and buildings, and they did considerable damage. They fought as far as Pskov. The men of Pskov and Novgorod went out to fight and a thousand Russians fell, but so did countless *Sosol'* (*The Pskov 3rd Chronicle*, year 1060).

These events put a temporary end to the Russians' military activities in coastal Estonia—their next raid mentioned in the chronicles did not happen until the start of the thirteenth century (Mägi 2018, 381–84). Nevertheless, in the twelfth century, the *Chud'* of inland Estonia and the Novgorod–Pskov princes mounted several military expeditions against each other.

The campaigns described in the Russian chronicles typically took place in winter, taking advantage of the paths running across the frozen earth, and the ice-bound rivers. In some cases, though, ships are mentioned sailing on northeastern Russia's large lakes. However, the princes of Kievan Rus had no fleet of warships on the Baltic Sea that would merit mention.

Changes along the Daugava Way

The Russian chronicles often speak of the *Chud'* and the related conflicts and confrontations in the context of the eleventh and twelfth centuries, completely overlooking any possible activities in the territories around the Daugava. This dearth of information could perhaps be explained by the absence of any chronicle-writing tradition in the Polotsk principality which held the Daugava Way to be within its sphere of interest. At any rate, some early thirteenth-century written sources place the Daugava basin within the Polotsk ambit. The Livs residing in the lower reaches of the river were apparently paying scat-tribute to the prince, while farther east, the Daugava waterway was controlled by the Jersika and Koknes principalities that were in turn partly dependent on Polotsk.

Judging by the above, and based on certain sagas and archaeological material, it seems safe to assume that the areas surrounding the Daugava Way were identified as a dominion of *Garðaríki*. No information is available, however, about the eleventh century, or any possible conflicts between the locals and the Slavic princes consolidating their power at the time. In 1106 the *Zimegola* (Semgallians) allegedly destroyed a large army of Polotsk princes (*The Primary Chronicle*, year 1106 (6614)). Meanwhile, Latgallia is first mentioned in 1200 when the combined forces of Novgorod and its allies plundered a region called *Lotygala* (*The Chronicle of Novgorod*, year 1200 (7708)).

The Latgallian strongholds of Koknes and Jersika have been archaeologically excavated along with their adjacent settlements. Jersika is thought to have functioned as the centre of a larger principality with many other hill-forts gracing its countryside. It has been hypothesized that the rulers of Jersika and Koknes adopted the Orthodox faith, and a building dating from the end of the twelfth century at the Jersika hill-fort has even been interpreted as an Orthodox church.[28] It remains unclear, however, whether these regions became dependent on the Polotsk principality in the twelfth century or somewhat earlier, towards the end of the Viking Age. The eleventh-century Latgallian burials are characterized by rich grave goods but the role of imports in their unique culture remained rather modest throughout, so it is unclear how much connection there was with Scandinavia, or Polotsk and areas further upstream along the Daugava (Fig. 11).[29]

The Livic region in the lower Daugava is rich in finds dating from the second half of the tenth century onwards, which have been recovered from large burial grounds and settlements (Fig. 12). It was also a period of prosperous hill-forts, most strikingly the complex of Daugmale, that included several cemeteries and open settlements. The site has yielded an extraordinary amount of varying craft-related products,

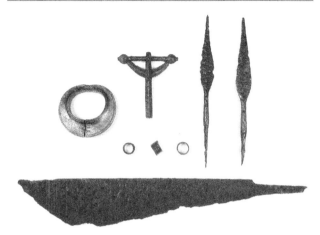

Figure 11. Latgallian grave goods from a male grave at Lejasbitēni inhumation cemetery, ninth to tenth century (LNVM A 11847:418-424). Photograph by R. Kaniņš. Courtesy of the National History Museum of Latvia.

nearly two hundred coins, and other items imported from the eastern and western territories alike (Radiņš 1998).[30]

Regrettably, the rushed rescue excavations at the settlements in the lower Daugava carried out in the middle of the twentieth century have been poorly published. These large settlements were partly fortified from the land side and consisted of buildings that formed a regular pattern or stood in groups.[31] The location across the river from Daugmale hill-fort and on the island of Dole suggests their function as semi-seasonal trading places where the population increased very substantially during the navigation season.

Links to international trade also seem to manifest themselves in the nearby Livic cemeteries which, unlike the contemporary Baltic Finnic cemeteries, included both inhumations and individual cremation burials. What strikes the eye in the female burials is the extraordinary number of graves furnished with jewellery hailing from neighbouring territories: more than one-third of the females buried in the grave-

Figure 12. Livian boy buried at burial no. 2 at Laukskola cemetery near Daugmale, eleventh century. Photograph by V. Ģinters (LVNM excavation reports AA 257). Courtesy of the National History Museum of Latvia.

yards surrounding Daugmale appear to be of non-Livic ethnicity. The material recovered from these cemeteries seems to imply females from Semgallia, Middle Sweden, Gotland, Couronia, Saaremaa, and inland Estonia, and individual Latgallian burials. With the exception of Semgallia and Latgallia, all these regions were part of the common cultural sphere of warriors—which makes men from the listed territories indistinguishable based on the grave goods alone. It is therefore fair to suggest that a similar ethnic diversity in fact also may have characterized the males buried in these cemeteries (Mägi 2018, 392–402).

The sudden rise in importance of the Daugava Way in eleventh-century trade is, likewise, marked with an increase in coin hoards later found almost everywhere around the river. It merits mention, however, that the amount of eleventh-twelfth century coins is nevertheless very much higher in Estonia than Latvia, as well as other Eastern Baltic regions. Based on the coin finds it can be concluded that the eleventh century saw the emergence of new trade routes which nonetheless did not eclipse the old, proven Viking Age ones.

The Last Baltic Sea Vikings

Written sources treat the eleventh and twelfth centuries much more extensively and in greater detail than the preceding periods. Sagas and chronicles provide far longer descriptions of Estonian and Couronian Vikings pillaging and plundering the Scandinavian coasts. Many researchers take this to indicate an unusual rise in the activity of Eastern Vikings from the eleventh century onwards. Since the period as a whole is characterized by a considerable upsurge in grave goods deposited with the burials all over the Eastern Baltic (Fig. 13), all too often conclusions have been drawn about the society becoming "wealthier". As a result, the eleventh and twelfth centuries are described by some researchers as the Baltics' "own Viking Age".

We disagree. Raids launched from the eastern shores of the Baltic Sea make a frequent appearance in the narratives about the Viking Age and earlier periods—nonetheless, these are hardly more than brief references. There is, sadly, a reckless tendency to overlook various tales speaking of *Austrvegr* or mentions of *Ruthenia* in Saxo's books. Dominated by maritime culture, these regions are without doubt at least partly identical with the Eastern Baltic and especially its northern half—not least topographically and geographically. The eleventh century witnessed a profusion of written sources by and large and this is why the later accounts of Eastern Vikings' pursuits are more numerous and also more detailed.

In the 1040s the Danish king Magnus the Good complained that Denmark was "much exposed to incursions of the Wends (*Vindi*), Couronians (*Kuri*) and other tribes along the Baltic, as well as of Saxons" (*The Saga of Magnús the Good*, chap. 23). A similar situation seems to have prevailed in the middle of the eleventh century when Canute the Holy, future king of Denmark, fought against the eastern Vikings (Saxo Grammaticus, 11.8). He is said to have achieved particular success during his kingship in the 1080s.

> King Knut was a strict and powerful ruler, who punished evildoers with great severity. During the reign of Harald

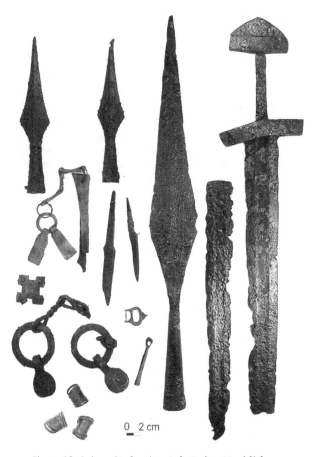

Figure 13. A deposit of male artefacts (cenotaph?) from
Viltina harbour site in Saaremaa, eleventh century
(Saaremaa Museum (SM) 10319). Photograph by M. Mägi.

Whetstone, however, there had been little in the way of punishment for outrages committed either by the Danes themselves, or by Vikings plundering in Denmark, such as Courlanders (*Kúrir*) and others from *Austrvegr*. After Knut came to power he defended the land fiercely and drove all the heathen not only from his land but from the very seas; so that because of Knut's authority and strength of arms, no Viking would dare lie off the coast of Denmark (*Knytlinga Saga*, chap. 29).

Despite the continued centralization of power in the eleventh and twelfth centuries, *jarls* or chieftains continued Viking-style raids to the Eastern Baltic. *Jarl* Erik of Denmark, for example, "sailed on Viking expeditions to *Austrvegr* fighting against the heathen, but allowed all Christians and merchants to go in peace wherever they might wish" (*Knytlinga Saga*, chap. 70). Even as late as 1185 Erik, Prince of Norway

had a large company, and as he was liberal to his men and had small revenues, his money fell short. The following winter he prepared to leave the country and sail to *Austrvegr* to plunder heathen lands. Many of the King's troops entered his service for this voyage, and he had five ships [...]. In the summer they sailed on *Austrvegr* to *Estland* and plundered *Vikar* and *Tunta*, and seized much booty (*Sverissaga*, chap. 113).

Scandinavian states undergoing a process of consolidation of royal power took protecting their shores very seriously and indeed achieved some success in organizing coastal defence throughout the eleventh and twelfth centuries. Early thirteenth-century sources habitually describe the raids of Couronians and coastal Estonians to the Swedish and Danish shores (for instance, in Henricus Lettus, VII:1), yet more effective coastal defence must have made such incursions—if the freebooters were small in number—an increasingly risky business.

Whenever assaults from the east warrant a more detailed account in twelfth- and thirteenth-century chronicles, it appears they usually involved multiple ships and several hundreds of men. In some cases—for example, in 1170, a three-hundred-strong force of Couronians (and Estonians) was badly defeated by the Danes at Blekinge in southern Sweden—it is not unlikely that the Estonians and Couronians were acting as allies of the Swedish in the then ongoing conflict between Denmark and Sweden (Mägi 2018, 360–62). In 1203, around five hundred men—judging by the number of ships attending—from Saaremaa ravaged southern Sweden, and in 1210 German pilgrims engaged in a battle with a 240-strong band of Couronians near Gotland (Henricus Lettus, VII:1–2; XIV: 1).

Viking expeditions departing from all coasts around the Baltic Rim thus continued, in some measure, throughout the eleventh and twelfth centuries. However, the mid-eleventh century world was not the same as a hundred or a hundred and fifty years before. Much had changed: the political situation in the neighbouring countries, mutual relations, trade routes, and the cultural landscape, and all this is adequately mirrored in the archaeological material recovered from the Eastern Baltic. In the Baltics, the eleventh and twelfth centuries constituted a whole new epoch, the final period of what is considered by them to be their prehistory; but that later history is a story for another day.

Notes

[26] See also Nils Blomkvist, "Early Agents of Europanization: Nicholas and Fulco on the Bumpy Road to Twelfth-Century Estonia," in *Sõnasse püütud minevik in honorem Enn Tarvel*, ed. Priit Raudkivi and Marten Seppel (Tallinn: Argo, 2009), 29–58.

27 The text is somewhat changed according to *Drevneskandinavskiye istochniki*, 70–71.

[28] Roberts Spirģis, "Archaeological Evidence on the Spread of Christianity to the Lower Daugava Area (10th–13th century)," in *Rome, Constantinople and Newly-Converted Europe. Archaeological and Historical Evidence*, vol. 1, ed. Maciej Salamon, Marcin Wołoszyn, Alexander Musin, and Perica Špehar (Kraków: Polish Academy of Sciences, 2012) and references.

[29] Arnis Radiņš, *10.–13. gadsimta senkapi Latgalu apdzivotaja teritorija un Austrumlatvijas etniskas, socialas un politiskas vestures jau-*

tajumi, Latvijas vēstures muzeja raksti: Arheologija 5 (Riga, N.I.M.S., 1999), 169–84.

[30] See also Zemītis, "10th–12th Century Daugmale," in *Cultural Interaction Between East and West*, ed. Fransson, 279–84.

[31] Andris Šnē, "Social Structures of Livonian Society in the Late Iron Age," 183–207 (see note 2 above).

Conclusion

The Viking Age in the Eastern Baltic is a subject that has frequently been treated in a national romantic vein, with a spotlight on the archaeologically rich eleventh and twelfth centuries. The so-called Viking Age "proper" is often overshadowed by the closing centuries of what is considered in the region as prehistory, and the researchers in the Baltic States and Finland focusing on this period are few and far between. This book has suggested some reasons why the ninth and tenth centuries are under-researched in Eastern Baltic archaeology.

Perhaps the paramount reason for this gap is the Baltic Finnic funeral tradition that did not include any grave goods until the second half of the tenth century. Another major factor was without doubt the political situation prevailing in the twentieth century (and even earlier) that resisted the inclusion of Estonian and Latvian archaeological material in international studies. Linguistic and cultural differences between the regions of the Eastern Baltic have also discouraged a cross-regional approach, and research is predominantly fixated on the researcher's native country or language-group area.

As shown in this book, the Viking Age Eastern Baltic could indeed be divided into two larger spheres based on their language and the concomitant culture: the Baltic Finnic and the Baltic. Viking Age trade, the role of the maritime element in the local culture, contacts, and cultural influences from east and west all functioned differently in these spheres. Recognition of this is crucial if we want to have an adequate picture of the processes operating in the Viking Age Baltic Rim.

We have also shown the crucial role in interpreting the eastern expansion of Viking Age Scandinavia of the common cultural sphere of warriors that emerged in the East Scandinavian and Baltic Finnic coastal areas. This shared cultural milieu dates back to the centuries preceding the Viking Age, and was evidently based on not just raids on each other but also on close personal contacts, adopted values, and beliefs. Archaeologically, the shared cultural milieu of warriors renders it somewhat difficult to decipher what is a "Scandinavian character" in the eastern territories, thus illustrating the international and multicultural nature of the processes at work during the period.

We have also seen the important sphere of shared cultural values spreading along the coastal regions, and the much stronger local colour characterizing the inland areas of the Eastern Baltic. Moreover, a clear distinction must be made between the regions dominated by the shared warrior culture and the southern part of the Eastern Baltic where isolated Scandinavian colonies thrived on the coast while local culture persisted without succumbing to any notable western influences.

We hope to have demonstrated above all that the Viking Age, across its decidedly diverse centuries, has played a powerful role in the Baltic States and in Finland. The whole region constituted a sort of a buffer zone between east and west, between Scandinavia and (later) Russia. Several processes characterizing the period—for example the emergence and development of trade centres, or struggles over spheres of influence—were directly mirrored in Eastern Baltic archaeological material.

The Eastern Baltic was emphatically part of the Viking world, and no interpretation of the activities of Vikings can be complete without attention to this region. Inclusion of the Baltic Finnic and Baltic archaeological material along with topographical and logistical factors in further research into the Vikings' eastern expansion will provide a better under-standing of the changes permeating the whole Viking Age, the epoch that played such a crucial role in patterning what is now Northern Europe.

Further Reading

This list only includes publications in English, although a great part of books and articles about the Viking Age Eastern Baltic have been written in other languages. Several of them may not be available for Anglophone readers. Therefore, mainly articles published in online journals have been selected. In most cases I have preferred publications from the last two decades.

Most of the topics addressed in this book have been thoroughly discussed and provided with references in Mägi, *In Austrvegr*. This list offers some essential sources and publications for further study.

Callmer, Johan. "The Archaeology of the Early Rus' c. AD 500–900." *Medieval Scandinavia* 13 (2000): 7–63.

> In this essay the early stages of *Rus'* are discussed with a focus on migration, assimilation, and acculturation. Callmer argues that a leading role in early Scandinavians' eastern expansion was played by the mixed Scandinavian-Finnic population and particularly the Åland archipelago.

Cultural Interaction Between East and West: Archaeology, Artefacts and Human Contacts in Northern Europe. Edited by Ulf Fransson, Marie Svedin, Sophie Bergerbrant, and Fedir Androshchuk. Stockholm: Stockholm University, 2007.

> This collection consists of multi-disciplinary articles, but several treat east-west contacts over the Baltic Sea in the Viking Age as well as in the periods before and afterwards. Several articles discuss Viking Age sites in the Eastern Baltic, such as Daugmale hill-fort,

Scandinavian artefacts found in the east, or the expansion of eastern Vikings to Russia.

Duczko, Wladislaw. *Viking Rus: Studies on the Presence of Scandinavians in Eastern Europe*. Leiden: Brill, 2004.

A good overview of Scandinavian influence in present-day northeastern Russia, Belarus, and Ukraine through archaeological as well as historical evidence. The author presents new theories for the origin of *Rus'* and the beginning of the *Rus'* state.

Fibula, Fabula, Fact: The Viking Age in Finland. Edited by Joonas Ahola and Frog with Clive Tolley. Helsinki: Finnish Literature Society, 2014.

Presents the latest results of Viking Age studies in Finland, including articles from fields including folklore studies, archaeology, linguistics, and genetics.

Gosden, Chris. *Archaeology of Colonialism: Cultural Contact from 5000 BC to the Present*. Cambridge: Cambridge Archaeology Press, 2004.

Recommended for readers who wish to learn more about different modes of cultural contacts. Similar developments also patterned the interaction between Scandinavians and the different peoples east of the Baltic Sea.

Hraundal, Thorir Jonsson. *The Rus in Arabic Sources: Cultural Contacts and Identity*. Doctoral dissertation. Bergen: Centre for Medieval Studies, University of Bergen, 2013. https://www.academia.edu/4094697/Rus_in_Arabic_Sources_Cultural_Contacts_and_Identity_PhD_dissertation, accessed September 25, 2018.

Offers an unconventional interpretation for the term Rus, discussing mainly how this ethnonym was used in written sources depicting today's southern Russia.

Identity Formation and Diversity in the Early Medieval Baltic and Beyond: Communicators and Communication. Edited by Johan Callmer, Ingrid Gustin, and Mats Roslund. Leiden: Brill, 2017.

> Ten scholars from different countries around the Baltic Sea discuss topics connected with overseas interactions and expressions of identities in the Viking Age Baltic Rim.

Jets, Indrek. "Scandinavian Late Viking Age Art Styles as a Part of the Visual Display of Warriors in 11th-century Estonia." *Estonian Journal of Archaeology* 16, no. 2 (2012): 118–39. http://www.kirj.ee/public/Archaeology/2012/issue_2/arch-2012-2-118-139.pdf, accessed September 26, 2018.

> An examination of Scandinavian animal-style ornamentation that decorates mainly weapons and belt fittings from Viking Age Estonia, Finland, and Latvia. The basic idea of the writing is that warriors of these countries used the ornament for reinforcing their identity shared with the eastern Vikings in Sweden and Denmark.

Jets, Indrek, and Mägi, Marika. "Local Shape, Foreign Decoration. Shared Culture Values in pre-Viking Period Baltic Rim as Indicated in the Decoration of Triangular-Headed Pins." *Fornvännen* 2015, no. 4 (2015): 257–66. http://samla.raa.se/xmlui/bitstream/handle/raa/9989/2015_257.pdf?sequence=1&isAllowed=y, accessed September 25, 2018.

> The article takes into consideration archaeological evidence that demonstrates the formation of the shared warrior culture along the coasts of the northern Baltic Sea.

Lehtosalo-Hilander, Pirkko-Liisa. *Luistari III. A Burial-Ground Reflecting the Finnish Viking Age Society.* Helsinki: Suomen Muinaismuistoyhdistys, 1982.

> An English overview of different visions about Finnish prehistoric society up to the 1980s, that presents an interpretation of seventh to twelfth-century social structures at the well-investigated inhumation cemetery at Luistari in Finland.

Mägi, Marika. *In Austrvegr: The Role of the Eastern Baltic in Viking Age Communication across the Baltic Sea.* Leiden: Brill, 2018.

> Discusses Viking Age Eastern Baltic and Finland from a trans-regional perspective, using predominantly archaeological evidence using written sources, topographic, and logistic approaches.

Pushkina, Tamara. "Viking Period pre-Urban Settlements in Russia and Finds of Artefacts of Scandinavian Character." In *Land, Sea and Home. Proceedings of conference on Viking-Period Settlement, at Cardiff, July 2001*, edited by John Hines, Alan Lane, and Mark Redknap, 41–53. Leeds: Maney, 2004.

> The essay discusses early urban settlements and artefacts indicating Scandinavian influence in present-day Russia, with a special focus on how to distinguish Scandinavian colonists from local people using foreign artefacts for expressing their social status.

Radiņš, Arnis. "Some Notes on the Daugava Way. The End of 12th—Beginning of 13th Century: Time of Changes on the Lower Daugava." In *Culture Clash or Compromise? The Europeanisation of the Baltic Sea Area 1100-1400 AD.* Edited by Nils Blomkvist, 178–91. Visby: Gotland Centre for Baltic Studies, 1998.

> The article treats one of the most relevant trade routes through the Eastern Baltic, the River Daugava, mainly discussing the development of this water route and peoples inhabiting the areas along the river.

Sayers, William. "A Glimpse of Medieval Curonian Vernacular Architecture in Egils Saga Skallagrímssonar." *Journal of Baltic Studies* 44, no. 3 (2013): 363–74. https://www.tandfonline.com/doi/abs/10.1080/01629778.2012.737506, accessed September 25, 2018.

> In this article the translation of the story from Egil's Saga into modern English is combined with a detailed overview of the cultural situation of Viking Age Couronia.

Šnē, Andris. "The Economy and Social Power in the Late Prehistoric Chiefdoms of Eastern Latvia." *Archaeologia Baltica*
6 (2006): 68–78. http://briai.ku.lt/downloads/AB/06/06_068-
079_Sne.pdf, accessed September 25, 2018.

> A putative reconstruction of Livic society in late prehistoric Latvia,
> discussing how economic advantages could have been used by local
> chieftains for reinforcing their social status.

*Transformatio Mundi. The Transition from the Late Migration
Period to the Early Viking Age in the East Baltic.* Edited by
Mindaugas Bertašius. Kaunas: Kaunas University of Technol-
ogy, Department of Philosophy and Cultural Science, 2006.

> The book includes works of archaeologists from nearly all the coun-
> tries around the Baltic Sea. Several of the articles treat issues con-
> nected with the Viking Age in the Eastern Baltic, especially the trade
> routes running through the region.

*The Viking Age in Åland. Insights into Identity and Remnants
of Culture.* Edited by Joonas Ahola, Frog, and Jenni Lucenius.
Helsinki: Academia Scientiarum Fennica, 2014.

> The Viking Age Åland archipelago between Sweden and Finland,
> which flourished up to the early eleventh century.

Virse, Ingrīda Liga, and Ritums, Ritvars. "The Grobiņa Complex of Dwelling Locations and Burial Sites, and Related
Questions." *Archaeologia Baltica* 17 (2012): 34–42. http://
briai.ku.lt/downloads/AB/17/17_034-042_Virse,_Ritums.pdf,
accessed September 25, 2018.

> Two Latvian archaeologists discuss recent excavations in Grobiņa,
> where a Scandinavian colony existed in the pre-Viking and early
> Viking periods.

*Wulfstan's Voyage: The Baltic Sea Region in the Early Viking
Age as Seen from Shipboard.* Edited by Anton Englert and
Athena Trakadas. Roskilde: The Viking Ship Museum in
Roskilde, 2009.

> Using the ninth-century travelogue by Wulfstan as a starting point,
> a number of prominent linguists, archaeologists, and historians dis-

cuss cultural interaction, trading centres and routes in the southeastern Baltic Sea region.

Zilmer, Kristel. *"He Drowned in Holmr's Sea—His Cargo-Ship Drifted to the Sea-Bottom, Only Three Came out Alive."* Records and Representations of Baltic Traffic in the Viking Age and the Early Middle Ages in Early Nordic Sources. Dissertationes Philologiae Scandinavicae Universitatis Tartuensis 1. Tartu: Tartu University Press, 2005. https://dspace.ut.ee/handle/10062/741, accessed September 25, 2018.

A thorough linguistic overview of how different place-names in the eastern coast of the Baltic Sea are mentioned on rune-stones.

Printed and bound by CPI Group (UK) Ltd, Croydon, CR0 4YY

25/03/2025

14647339-0002